MATT AND TOM O

ULTIMATE FOOTBALL HEROES

MESSI

FROM THE PLAYGROUND
TO THE PITCH

DINO

First published by Dino Books in 2017,
An imprint of Bonnier Books UK,
The Plaza,
535 Kings Road,
London SW10 0SZ

@dinobooks
@footieheroesbks
www.heroesfootball.com
www.bonnierbooks.co.uk

Text © Matt and Tom Oldfield 2017
The right of Matt and Tom Oldfield to be identified as the authors of this work has been
asserted by them in accordance with the copyright, designs and patents act 1988.

Design by www.envydesign.co.uk

All rights reserved. No part of this publication may be reproduced, stored in a
retrieval system, or transmitted in any form or by any means, without the prior
permission in writing of the publisher, nor be otherwise circulated in any form
of binding or cover other than that in which it is published and without a similar
condition including this condition being imposed on the subsequent purchaser.

Paperback ISBN: 978 1 78606 403 5
E-book ISBN: 978 1 78606 837 8

British Library cataloguing-in-publication data:
A catalogue record for this book is available from the British Library.

Printed and bound in Great Britain by Clays Lltd, Elcograf S.p.A.

12

All names and trademarks are the property of their respective owners, which
are in no way associated with Dino Books. Use of these names does not imply any
cooperation or endorsement.

For Noah and Nico,
Southampton's future strikeforce.

ULTIMATE
FOOTBALL HEROES

Matt Oldfield is an accomplished writer and the editor-in-chief
of football review site Of Pitch & Page. Tom Oldfield is a freelance
sports writer and the author of biographies on Cristiano Ronaldo,
Arsène Wenger and Rafael Nadal.

Cover illustration by Dan Leydon.
To learn more about Dan visit danleydon.com
To purchase his artwork visit etsy.com/shop/footynews
Or just follow him on Twitter @danleydon

TABLE OF CONTENTS

ACKNOWLEDGEMENTS

First of all, I'd like to thank John Blake Publishing –
and particularly my editor James Hodgkinson – for
giving me the opportunity to work on these books
and for supporting me throughout. Writing stories for
the next generation of football fans is both an honour
and a pleasure.

I wouldn't be doing this if it wasn't for Tom. I owe
him so much and I'm very grateful for his belief in
me as an author. I feel like Robin setting out on a
solo career after a great partnership with Batman. I
hope I do him (Tom, not Batman) justice with these
new books.

Next up, I want to thank my friends for keeping

me sane during long hours in front of the laptop. Pang, Will, Mills, Doug, John, Charlie – the laughs and the cups of coffee are always appreciated.

I've already thanked my brother but I'm also very grateful to the rest of my family, especially Melissa, Noah and of course Mum and Dad. To my parents, I owe my biggest passions: football and books. They're a real inspiration for everything I do.

Finally, I couldn't have done this without Iona's encouragement and understanding during long, work-filled weekends. Much love to you.

CHAPTER 1

TREBLE TIME

'Hey, how's it going?' Lionel said, giving his fellow Argentinian Carlos Tevez a big hug as they waited in the tunnel.

Lionel was about to play in the 2014–15 Champions League final but he wasn't nervous at all. It was the third time he had played in the final with Barcelona and he had won both times before. He was a born winner and he was the best player in the world. So he felt very confident as he walked out on to the pitch at the Olympiastadion in Berlin to face Italian giants Juventus.

Lionel looked up into the stands and saw the huge wall of red and blue, or '*azulgrana*' as they called it in Spanish – the colours representing Barcelona, one of the world's biggest clubs and Lionel's home since the age of thirteen. He had played in some amazing Barcelona teams but this was perhaps the best team of all. They had already won the Spanish League and the Spanish Cup – now could they win the Champions League to make it an incredible Treble?

'Yes we can!' they cheered together.

Lionel's old friends Gerard Piqué and Javier Mascherano were the rocks in defence, Andrés Iniesta and Xavi controlled the midfield, while 'MSN' scored the goals up front. That's what the media were calling the world's best ever strikeforce – Lionel Messi, the Uruguayan Luis Suárez, and the Brazilian Neymar. Together, they had scored 120 goals already, with one big game left to play.

'Come on!' Lionel shouted as they waited for kick-off. When he was younger, he was too shy to speak to his teammates but he was twenty-seven now and one of their leaders.

Within four minutes, Neymar passed to Andrés, who passed to Ivan Rakitić, who scored. Barcelona were 1-0 up. They made everything look so easy with their quick, passing football, and Lionel hadn't even been involved – but he knew how important teamwork was.

'Great work!' he shouted to Ivan. Even he couldn't do everything on his own.

Playing just behind Neymar and Luis, Lionel kept searching for the space to work his magic. He was known as The Flea, buzzing around everywhere and terrorising his opponents. With his close control, quick feet and footballing brain, he only ever needed one second. Especially in his favourite spot: just outside the penalty area on the right side, he could dribble with his amazing left foot. Lionel loved scoring goals but he loved creating goals too – there was nothing he couldn't do.

Barcelona were playing well but in the second half, Juventus equalised. Just when his team needed him most, Lionel came alive. He passed to Neymar, who flicked it back to Lionel, who passed to Luis, who passed back to Lionel. His shot went wide but 'MSN' were looking dangerous.

'If we keep this up, we'll score again!' Lionel told the others.

Minutes later, he dribbled forward again. The defender tried to tackle him but Lionel was too quick and too skilful. When he grabbed his shirt, Lionel shrugged him off. He wasn't the biggest footballer but he had worked hard to build up his strength.

As Lionel flew towards goal, Neymar made a run to make space for him. On the edge of the penalty area, Lionel decided to shoot. The ball flew straight at the goalkeeper but it swerved and dipped and he couldn't hold on to it. Luis sprinted towards the ball and smashed it into the net. 2-1!

As Luis jumped the advertising board, Lionel and Neymar were right behind him. It was yet another 'MSN' goal and Barcelona were one step closer to another Champions League trophy.

'There's plenty of time to score another!' Neymar said with a big smile on his face. Their favourite form of defence was attack.

In injury time, a clearance fell to Lionel. He looked up and saw his Brazilian teammate sprinting forward.

Stretching out his leg, he played a perfect through-ball. Neymar and Luis had a two-on-one against the Juventus centre-back. Neymar passed to Luis and as the defender moved across, Luis passed it back to Neymar. His shot rocketed into the bottom corner. 3-1! Barcelona were the Champions of Europe.

At the final whistle, Lionel hugged Andrés and Xavi. Together, they had conquered the football world again. He was so grateful to his amazing teammates. Their clever passes always arrived at his feet, no matter where he was on the pitch.

'After my injuries last year, some people thought that my best days were over,' Lionel said. 'They were so wrong!'

In the 2014/15 season he had helped Barcelona win the Treble with 58 goals and 25 assists in only 57 games. He was very proud of his return to form.

As Xavi lifted the trophy into the air, Lionel was right at the centre of the celebrations. He hadn't scored a goal in the final this time round, but he had still played a very important role.

'Thiago!' Lionel called to his three-year-old son,

who was wearing a Barcelona shirt with '10 MESSI' on the back. He kissed his girlfriend Antonella and carried Thiago around the pitch to wave to the fans. His little family meant the world to him.

'Look, there's your Grandpa and Grandma!' Lionel said to Thiago, pointing to Jorge and Celia in the crowd.

Without the love and support of his parents, Lionel wouldn't have made the brave move from Argentina to Spain to chase his dream of playing professional football. He had arrived at Barcelona as a tiny teenager with amazing natural talent but some of his coaches had their doubts. Did he really have the strength and desire to make it to the very top?

Nearly fifteen years later, the answer was there in Lionel's trophy cabinet: seven La Liga titles, four Champions League trophies, four FIFA Ballon d'Or trophies and one Olympic Gold Medal. He was the best player in the world but The Flea had plenty more magic up his sleeve.

CHAPTER 2

JORGE'S DREAM

Jorge Messi stood on his doorstep and slowly rocked his newborn son in his arms. It was a warm, sunny afternoon in Argentina and Jorge had stories to share with him.

'Welcome to La Bajada, Lionel,' he said quietly. 'This will always be your home. You'll love it here – it's a nice and peaceful community. The people are very friendly and the kids play freely in the streets. Plus, all of your family live nearby: your grandparents, your aunts and uncles, and your cousins too.

'I built this house myself with my father – your grandfather, Eusebio. He worked as a builder and he taught me all of his skills. The house is nothing special but it will do for now, until your brothers Rodrigo and Matías want their own bedrooms, and then so will you!

'What else shall I tell you? Your great-grandparents came to Argentina from Italy and Spain a long time ago. So our culture is a real mix of Europe and South America. And luckily for you, your grandmother Celia makes the best pasta dishes in the world!

'Just before you were born, we nearly moved to Australia. There are lots of good jobs there but in the end, we couldn't bear to leave our family behind. It's strange to think that you might have grown up speaking English as well as Spanish, and you might have become a surfer or a cricketer! But don't worry, you're an Argentinian and so you will be a footballer instead.

'As you'll soon find out, this whole country is football-mad. When Diego Maradona lifted the World Cup for Argentina last summer, the party went on for weeks! And Rosario is a particularly special place. So many great Argentinian footballers have come from this city. Maybe you will be the next!'

Celia tiptoed into the room. 'Is he asleep yet?' she whispered.

Jorge nodded and gave a big thumbs-up. When his wife left the room, he continued.

'Let me tell you the story about your name. I'm sure you'll hear it many times during your life! Your mum loved "Leonel" with two "e"s and I liked it too. But as I went to register your name, I thought about how people would shorten it. I really don't like "Leo" – don't ask me to explain why!

'So I asked for a list of other names and I found the English spelling – "Lionel", with an "i" instead of an "e". "Lio" – that sounds much better to me. When I got home and told her, your mum was so angry with me! I don't think she'll let me make a decision like that ever again. But soon she'll love your name just as much as me. It's a special name for a special boy. Now let's get back to football. I'm afraid you won't have a choice about what team you support – our family are all "Lepers", fans of the best local team, Newell's Old Boys. When I was younger, I played for their youth team. I was a pretty good central midfielder but then I had to go away for military service and when I returned, I married your mum and then Rodrigo and Matías were born. I didn't have time to play at a high level anymore – I needed to earn money to feed my growing family.

'So I got a good job as a factory manager but I still play football every now and again. Soon, you'll come and watch me play and hopefully you'll be proud of your dad. One of you will play for Newell's Old Boys – I'm sure of it! That was my dream and now I'm passing it on to my sons.'

Jorge pointed across the road to a small grassy area.

'For the first few years, that will be your stadium. You'll have your first football battles there with your brothers and your friends. You'll get your first cuts and bruises and you'll score your first goals. Then, you'll move on to the youth football pitches at Newell's and when you're ready, you'll make your debut at their stadium, *El Coloso del Parque*. You'll become a local legend – no pressure!

'There is no better feeling in the world than hearing thousands of fans chanting your name. Everyone wants to be a hero. If you work hard, you can achieve any goals. But first, get some sleep!'

CHAPTER 3

FIRST STEPS

When he was nine months old, Lionel took his first, wobbly steps.

'That's it, steady now!' Celia cheered as she waited to catch him if he fell.

Lionel giggled and moved his little legs faster. He was free!

Once he was a confident walker, the family had to keep a very close eye on him. In La Bajada, people always left their front doors open and one day, he walked right out into the street.

'Lionel, stop!' Jorge shouted as he chased after him. 'It's dangerous!'

There wasn't usually much traffic in the

neighbourhood but as Lionel stepped out, a boy rushed past on a bicycle and knocked him over. After the shock of the fall, he cried and cried.

'You're safe, son,' Jorge kept saying, hugging Lionel tight. 'You gave us quite a scare there. Please promise me you won't do that again!'

On his first birthday, Lionel got his first Newell's Old Boys kit. It was so big for him that it looked like a dress.

'You're a proper fan now!' Jorge told him with a big smile on his face. They took photos for the family collection.

Lionel wore the red-and-black shirt every day and he became upset when it had to be washed. Jorge was delighted to see his son's growing interest in football.

'He'll be playing with Rodrigo and Matías in no time!' Jorge told his wife excitedly.

'Maybe that will tire him out a bit,' Celia replied with a sigh. 'He never stops running around at the moment.'

When his brothers went out to play, Lionel

followed behind with his grandmother. He loved watching football but he really wanted to be playing. That was the next step.

On his third birthday, Lionel got the best present ever – a brand new football.

'Amazing, thanks!' he shouted out, giving his parents big hugs. 'It's beautiful!'

'And it's about as big as you!' Rodrigo joked. It was a size 5 and Lionel could barely hold it in his little hands.

'Come on, let's go and have a kickabout!' Jorge cheered and they all crossed the road to play.

The ball came up above Lionel's knee but he controlled it well and, with light touches, he dribbled towards goal. There was a very serious look on his face as he kicked it with all his power. Jorge was always going to let it in but the ball went right in the corner.

'Wow, you're a natural!' Matías cheered as they lifted Lionel up into the air to celebrate his first goal.

The ball went everywhere with Lionel: sometimes in his arms but usually at his feet. He even slept with it in his bed. His brothers liked to tease him – 'How's your best friend?' – but he didn't care. He was getting better and better.

When Lionel turned four, his mum finally let him go and play with his brothers in their local matches.

'Look after him!' Celia shouted to Rodrigo and Matías as they rushed out of the house.

From the window of their house, she kept an eye on her youngest son but she didn't need to worry. Lionel ran and ran, snapping at defenders' heels like an excited puppy. When he got the ball, he kept it simple with neat passes to his new teammates. He didn't want them to think he was a show-off.

'You're doing well! Now try one of your dribbles,' Matías suggested.

Lionel waited patiently until he spotted a gap in the defence. Then with a burst of speed, he dribbled between two defenders and passed it to his teammate Javier to score.

'Great work, Titch!' Javier laughed. Lionel didn't really like his new nickname but it was nice to have one. It added to his growing confidence on the pitch.

Lionel was much smaller and younger than his opponents but they still couldn't get the ball off him. It was as if it was glued to his foot. Eventually, they got frustrated and kicked him.

Owwwwww!

If it was really painful, Lionel did sometimes cry but he always got back up and carried on.

'How's the ankle?' Rodrigo asked him. He was following his mum's orders. 'Do you want to rest it for a bit?

Lionel shook his head. 'No, it's fine. I want to win!'

He loved the challenge of playing against older kids, but playing with his own friends was fun too. He didn't need to worry so much about getting hurt and it was nice to escape from his brothers for a bit. The pitch became a magical space for their fun football adventures.

'What shall we play today?' Lionel asked the other players. 'A penalty shoot-out? World Cup Doubles? Three versus three?'

'How about the five of us versus you?!' Walter suggested with a big grin on his face.

'No, I'd still win!' Lionel laughed.

'Not if we tie your feet together!' Diego argued.

Once they became hungry, most of his friends headed home for dinner but Lionel always stayed behind to practise. His mum didn't have far to go to find him.

'I won't tell you again – the food is getting cold,' Celia shouted from the doorstep. 'If you're not at the table in one minute, I'll give your dinner to Matías!'

'Coming!' Lionel replied.

CHAPTER 4

GRANDOLI

'When can I join Grandoli?' Lionel asked Jorge. If he asked enough times, surely his dad would give in and let him play. That was his big plan.

Grandoli Football Club played their matches at the end of the road that the Messi family lived on. The pitch was poor, with stones and bits of glass in amongst the mud. The teams only played in the evenings because a school used the pitch during the day, and the lighting wasn't good at all. But at least Grandoli was a proper team with a proper kit. And Rodrigo and Matías already played there.

'Okay, I'll take you to training tomorrow,' Jorge said eventually when his youngest son turned five.

Lionel jumped into the air. His time had come. He couldn't wait for 'baby football', the seven-a-side game that young Argentinians played until they turned eleven. All of his training on the pitch next to his house would finally be put to the test.

'Thanks Dad, I'm ready for this!'

Salvador Aparicio was the coach of Lionel's age group, the team all born in 1987. He had seen Lionel at Grandoli before, when the boy had watched his older brothers play, but it was only as he practiced keepy-uppies before training in his massive red-and-white shirt that Salvador realised just how small he was. Most of his new teammates towered over him.

'The most skilful players are often very small,' the coach told himself. 'And he's got plenty of time to grow!'

Salvador liked his players to have fun, both in training and in matches. It was very important for youngsters to enjoy their football and not get too stressed about fitness and tactics.

'Right kids – let's start with a few *rondos*!'

Rondos were the South American version of piggy

in the middle. It was an entertaining way for the team to improve their control, balance and passing. Lionel was already brilliant at all three, and after fifteen minutes, he still hadn't made any mistakes.

'Wow, his touch is incredible!' Salvador said to one of the other coaches.

In the game at the end of training, Lionel wasn't a selfish show-off – that wasn't his style. He had a lot of the ball but he dribbled and passed patiently, waiting for the right opportunity to create a goal. In thirty minutes of football, he didn't lose possession once and he scored ten goals.

'That kid's got a very special gift,' Salvador told Lionel's grandmother, Celia. He loved discovering great new talents and this new player was the best he'd ever seen.

'I know – you can thank us later!' she replied. 'Lionel, come on, it's time to go home now!'

Lionel sighed and dragged himself away from his own shooting exercises. He was the last one left on the pitch but he could have stayed out there for hours. If he didn't practise, he wouldn't become perfect.

The team trained three times a week and then played matches every Saturday. It was a lot of football but it was never enough for Lionel. He was always hungry for more. At Las Heras Primary School, he sat in class waiting for the bell to ring. In between each lesson, they had a fifteen-minute break.

'Come on, let's go and play!' he yelled as they all ran to get the football.

Lionel was the best footballer and therefore the leader of the gang. In lessons, he was a quiet boy but with a football at his feet, he was a completely different character. No-one could get it off him as he danced around the playground. At first it was amazing to watch but soon, the other boys got frustrated and sometimes they complained to the teacher.

'Miss, Titch won't pass the ball!'

'What do you want me to do?' she replied, smiling. 'I can't tackle him either!'

On weekdays, Lionel's grandmother, Celia, picked him up from school, took him home for a biscuit and a glass of juice, and then took him to football. It was a routine that they both loved and soon Lionel's younger cousin, Emanuel, joined them too.

'With you in goal and me in attack, no-one will be able to beat us!' Lionel said happily.

It was true. The more Lionel played, the better he became, and Grandoli hardly lost a game. Sometimes, he dribbled around the whole team to score. Defenders tried everything to stop him – kicking him, pushing him, elbowing him, and pulling his shirt – but it was no use.

'Keep going, kid!' Salvador told Lionel if his head ever dropped. He didn't have much to teach his superstar. He just encouraged him to play his natural, beautiful game.

With wondergoal after wondergoal, big crowds started to come and watch Lionel play. Sometimes, even his opponents clapped at his skills. People called him 'the next Maradona'.

Celia was a very proud grandparent as she cheered from the sidelines:

'Great save, Emanuel!'

'Referee – that should have been a penalty!'

'Pass it to Lionel – he'll score!'

Lionel was only six years old but he took football very seriously. Before every match, he prepared his boots carefully. He washed them with water, and then he cleaned them with a cloth and a brush until they sparkled.

'You're not a professional yet!' Matías joked.

'No, not *yet*!' Lionel replied with a cheeky grin. It was only a matter of time.

CHAPTER 5

FAMILY FUN

At the Messi family party each Sunday, the adults cooked and chatted, and the kids played football all day long. Lionel always looked forward to it – football and family were his two favourite things in the world.

There were five youngsters – Rodrigo, Matías and Lionel, and then their cousins Maxi and Emanuel. Lionel and Emanuel were much younger than the others but after their success together with the Grandoli Team of '87, they were feeling brave.

'This time, we'll play the two of us against the three of you!' Lionel suggested with his arm around his teammate's shoulder.

Rodrigo laughed. 'Are you sure about this? You

barely come up to my waist – we'll crush you!'

'We'll see about that!' Emanuel fought back. He would make the saves and Lionel would score the goals. They were a winning combination.

'This should be interesting,' Jorge said to Maxi and Emanuel's dad, Claudio. They moved a little closer to watch the match.

The boys used rocks for goalposts and once the pitch was laid out, they were ready to begin. The first team to score six goals would win the match.

Emanuel passed to Lionel and he flicked the ball around Maxi with ease. Now he just had his two brothers to beat. He slowed down a bit to think about his options. As Matías and Rodrigo both ran in for the tackle, Lionel quickly moved the ball to the left, then to the right and in a flash, he glided in between them. 1-0!

'How on earth did he do that?' Claudio asked in amazement.

Jorge shrugged – his son was a little magician. 'Nice work!' he cheered.

Soon it was 3-0 and Lionel's brothers were not

happy. The two youngsters were making them look like fools. What could they do to get back in the game? Lionel had the skill but they had the strength and so they used it. They started to push and kick him – it was the only way to get the ball off him.

'Matías, be careful with Leo!' Jorge shouted.

'It's not my fault that he's small and weak!' Matías replied angrily.

There was always fighting. While the match went on, they weren't family anymore; they were rivals. And they would do anything to win.

Lionel got up to take the free-kick. He was used to being fouled and he didn't let it upset him. Scoring was the best form of revenge. As Rodrigo ran back towards his goal, Lionel chipped the ball just over his head and in between the posts. 4-0!

The older boys fought back to 4-3 but Lionel didn't give up. He was a winner and losing wasn't an option. He scored to make it 5-3 but then Maxi and Matías scored to make it 5-5. It was one of the most exciting games they'd ever played.

'Next goal wins!' Claudio called from the sidelines.

Lionel needed to do something special but how? It was three versus two and they were marking him very tightly. As he passed to Emanuel, Lionel sprinted into space and when he got the ball back, he dribbled forward at speed. Matías backed away until he had no choice but to make a tackle. Just as he stretched his leg out, Lionel shifted the ball to the left. He was away! Rodrigo ran out of his goal to block the shot but Lionel put it through his legs.

Goooooooooooooooooaaaaaaaaaaaaaaaaaaallllllllllllll llllllllllllllllllllll!!!!!!!!!!!!!!!!!!!

As the losers lay down on the concrete, the winners celebrated a famous victory.

'What's the score?' their grandmother Celia asked from the front door.

'It's just finished,' Jorge told her. 'Lionel and Emanuel just beat the others.'

Celia wasn't surprised – she had been watching the Team of '87 for a long time. 'That's perfect timing because dinner's ready!'

As the boys came inside to wash their hands, the amazing smells of the spaghetti bolognese hit their nostrils. Suddenly they were really hungry and they raced to the table.

'Is that enough for you?' his grandmother asked, putting a huge plate of food in front of Lionel.

He shook his head. 'More please!'

After he'd had seconds and a quick rest on the sofa, he was ready to go again. 'How about another match?' he asked the others.

Rodrigo groaned. 'I'm not playing against you again today!'

Matías and Maxi agreed. They were too tired for that.

Emanuel had a better idea. 'Why don't we go down to the plaza instead? We can challenge some of the local boys to a match. No-one will beat the five of us!'

Lionel nodded eagerly. He loved the challenge of playing against new opponents, and it would be nice to play *with* his family, rather than against them.

When they got to the plaza, they asked a group of teenagers, who took one look and laughed.

'No way! We're not playing against *him*,' they said, pointing at Lionel. 'He's way too small!'

It was the Messi family's turn to laugh. 'Just wait until you see him play!'

CHAPTER 6

NEWELL'S

With Lionel's reputation spreading fast across Rosario, Salvador knew that he wouldn't be able to keep his star player at Grandoli for long. His brothers already played for Newell's, so it was only a matter of time before he joined them.

'They would be stupid not to take him right now,' Salvador told Jorge after yet another man-of-the-match performance. Grandoli would miss Lionel a lot but everyone knew that he needed to challenge himself at a bigger club.

A few weeks later, Newell's asked Lionel to play for them in a preseason tournament. It was the chance that he had been waiting for.

'If I do well, I'll be signing for my favourite team!' he told his grandmother Celia.

'If you play like you normally do, there's no way they won't sign you,' she told him. His grandmother was always his biggest fan.

Quique Domínguez was the coach of their Team of '87. He had seen Lionel play a few incredible games for Grandoli but only when he saw the boy playing alongside the talented Newell's youngsters did he realise just how special he was.

'Before today, I thought my team was good but he's so much better than everyone else!' Quique told the other coaches excitedly. 'He's the most gifted kid I've ever seen. I have to have that boy in my team.'

The other coaches agreed. 'We can't let him go! You can't teach that amazing technique – he was born with it.'

A month later, Lionel was a Newell's player. His dream had come true and he wasn't even seven years old yet. But he didn't get carried away. Las Malvinas, the Newell's youth team training centre, wasn't a huge football palace with all of the newest equipment; it was just a simple place with two pitches, an office and a cafeteria.

Every day as his dad dropped him off for training, Lionel looked at the mural showing the names of all of the Newell's legends. One day, he vowed, his name would be on that wall, but there was plenty more work to do first.

'I've seen the incredible talent that you have,' Quique told him on one of his first days at training. 'I promise that we won't change the way you play but we'll help you to improve your technique even further. And we'll give you a bit more of that Newell's mentality!'

Lionel was already a very competitive player but he quickly became a winning machine. The Team of '87 thrashed anyone that dared to play against them.

'Diego, play the pass now!' Lionel shouted as he made another great run behind the defence. The striker gave him the ball and he dribbled past the goalkeeper and scored. He made everything look so easy and natural.

A few minutes later, Lionel dribbled past three

defenders. He could have taken a shot but as the last defender came to block, he passed to Diego. All the striker had to do was beat the keeper. He did that every time.

Their partnership was perfect – Diego Rovira was tall and strong, and Lionel was small and quick. 'Little and Large' their teammates called them. Together, they scored goals for fun.

'How many have you got now?' Diego asked halfway through the season.

'About fifty?' Lionel guessed. 'Sorry, I've lost count!'

When defenders fouled or insulted Lionel, Diego was always there to protect him.

'Go and pick on someone your own size!' he told them. 'And someone as rubbish at football as you!'

Lionel loved playing with his teammates but he was always the star. Without him, the Newell's team fell apart. In one tournament, they made it all the way to the final. The prize was a set of brand new bikes for the members of the winning team.

'Perfect – my bike is really old and rusty,' Diego said with a big smile. 'Let's win this final!'

But just before kick-off, Lionel was nowhere to be seen. The players started to panic.

'Where could he be?'

'Is he injured?'

'What do we do without him?'

'Who's going to create our goals now?'

Lionel's teammates loved him because even though he was their best player by miles, he wasn't arrogant. He was a real team player. On the pitch, he didn't moan if someone played a bad pass and he wasn't lazy. In fact, he ran more than anyone.

'We need him!' they cheered.

After ten minutes of searching, the referee couldn't delay the match any longer. Newell's had to start without their leader and by half-time, they were losing 1-0.

'You've got to forget about Lionel for today,' Quique told his team on the side of the pitch. They needed to believe in themselves, and not just their superstar. 'We can do this without h–'

At that moment, Lionel came rushing up to them.

'Sorry I'm late!' he panted. 'I couldn't open the

toilet door, so in the end I had to smash the window! Are we winning?'

'No, but we'll win this now!' Diego laughed.

Their hero had returned just in time to save the day. Newell's won 3-1 and Lionel scored a hat-trick.

'Maybe we'll lock you in the toilets more often!' Quique joked as they celebrated.

'No, please don't!' the players all shouted.

With his football career going from strength to strength, Lionel had only one big worry in his life – his beloved grandmother Celia was very ill. At first, she just grew weaker but then she started to lose her memory.

'Grandma, it's me – Leo!' he told her, but she just smiled at him.

Lionel hated to see his grandmother looking so pale and confused. He remembered her on the touchline at Grandoli, full of life as she cheered him on and argued with the referees. Without her love and support, he definitely wouldn't have become such a brilliant player.

Just before his eleventh birthday, Lionel got the terrible news that he had feared – Celia had died.

'No!' he cried as his mum tried to comfort him. 'She didn't get to see me become a professional!'

'Son, she will always be watching you and cheering you on,' his mum promised him.

For a few days, Lionel was too upset to play football. But he knew that his grandmother wouldn't want him to stop. He had to get back out on the pitch and do her proud. When he scored a goal in his next match, he pointed to the sky with both hands and looked up.

'That one's for you, Grandma,' Lionel said, with tears in his eyes.

CHAPTER 7

LOVE AND FRIENDSHIP

'Let's go and play Playstation at my house,' Diego suggested after training.

'Cool, I'll be Real Madrid!' Gerardo Grighini shouted straight away.

'I'll be Barcelona!' Lionel said next. His favourite player was River Plate's Argentinian playmaker Pablo Aimar but Barcelona were a much better team. They had amazing attackers like Rivaldo and Luís Figo.

'That's not fair!' Lucas Scaglia complained. 'I always play as Barcelona – they're *my* team. Fine, today I'll be Manchester United.'

'And I'll be Juventus,' Diego said.

If they weren't playing football together on the

pitch for Newell's, the Team of '87 were often playing football video games together. Their loud, entertaining tournaments went on for hours. Lionel loved hanging out with his friends.

'You might be the best footballer in real life, Leo, but I can definitely beat you on FIFA!' Gerardo joked as they walked.

Despite Jorge's best efforts, Lionel was still called 'Leo' by all his friends, but they also still called him 'Titch' because he remained very small for his age. But he never let that stop him.

'I've got better balance because I'm closer to the ground,' he told his teammates. 'That's why I can change direction so easily when I'm dribbling. The doctor called it a "low centre of gravity".'

When they turned eleven years old, the Team of '87 moved from seven-a-side 'baby' football to the real thing – eleven-a-side football. Lionel was so excited.

'I'll be even better with the extra space,' he told Diego. 'I'll play just behind you and they won't be able to mark me because I'll run all over the pitch!'

The only bad thing about eleven-a-side football was that the defenders were bigger and stronger than ever. The other teams in the league knew all about Lionel's talent and they did everything they could to stop him – insults, kicks and pushes all game long. He had to be very alert in order to protect himself.

As he received the ball, Lionel could see the defender sliding in for the tackle out of the corner of his eye. In a flash, he flicked the ball to the left and escaped with it. The defender lay on the grass and watched as Newell's scored again.

'How did you know he was there?' Diego asked as they celebrated.

'I think I've got a sixth sense now!' Lionel laughed.

At Diego's house, they made snacks to eat while they played. Gerardo's Real Madrid beat Lionel's Barcelona, and then Lucas's Manchester United. In the final, they drew 2-2 with Diego's Juventus.

'Penalties!' they all cheered. It was the most exciting part of the game. Lionel was supporting Juventus and Lucas was supporting Real Madrid.

'It's a shame that one of these great sides has to lose this tense final,' Lucas said, acting out the role of commentator. Everyone laughed.

Gerardo's goalkeeper made two great saves to win the tournament for Real Madrid. He jumped around the room to celebrate.

'What shall we do now?' Diego asked. It wouldn't get dark for a few more hours.

'Why don't we see what your cousins are doing?' Gerardo said to Lucas with a big smile on his face.

Gerardo and Diego were always asking to meet Lucas's beautiful cousins Paula, Antonella and Carla. Lionel was too shy to ask but he liked the plan too.

'Okay, I'll check but only if you find a match for me as well!' Lucas told them.

Diego shook his head. 'Sorry mate, you're just too ugly!'

As they rolled around laughing, Lucas jumped on Diego and soon they were all play-fighting.

'What's all the noise?' Diego's mum asked from the doorway.

'Sorry!' they all replied.

'Why don't you go out and get some fresh air?' his mum suggested. 'Dinner won't be ready for about an hour.'

'Great idea! Thanks, Mrs Rovira,' Gerardo said politely.

They met up with Lucas's cousins in a café nearby. They had brought a friend along, so it was four boys and four girls. Diego chatted with Paula and Gerardo chatted with Carla. Lionel tried to speak to Antonella but he didn't know what to say. She was so pretty – why would she want to talk to *him*?

'So you play football with Lucas?' Antonella asked eventually after an awkward silence.

'Yes, we've been playing together since we were seven,' Lionel replied. What else should he say? 'Have you ever seen him play?'

It was a stupid question because Antonella clearly didn't care about football but she was nice enough to reply.

'No, not yet but Lucas says you're a really good player.'

Lionel's face went bright red. He didn't want to

boast. 'Yes, we've got a really good team. You should come and watch us!'

Antonella shrugged. 'Maybe.'

Lionel couldn't stop staring at her long, brown hair and her big, sparkling eyes. He was in love.

'She's way out of your league!' Gerardo told him on the walk back to Diego's house. 'Everyone in Rosario wants to marry her. I'm sorry but Antonella won't be interested in a tiny guy like you.'

'We'll see about that!' Lionel replied. Just like on the football pitch, he wasn't going to give up at the first sign of failure.

CHAPTER 8

GROWING PROBLEMS

'It's nice to meet you,' Dr Schwarzstein said, offering his hand. Lionel shook it but he was too shy to say anything. He was very glad to have his mum there with him – doctors were scary.

'I hear you're a very good footballer,' Dr Schwarzstein continued. 'Who do you support?'

Lionel was happy to answer questions about football. 'Newell's.'

'Good man – me too! Hopefully I'll get to watch you playing at *El Coloso del Parque* one day.'

Lionel suddenly looked sad. 'That's my dream but I really need to grow if I'm going to become a professional footballer.'

Dr Schwarzstein smiled. 'Don't worry – that's why you're here. I'm going to do some tests to see if there's anything we can do to help you grow taller. There's a chance that your body might not be producing some of the growth hormones that most people have.'

Lionel nodded and crossed his fingers. A month later, he returned to hear the test results.

'I've got good news and bad news,' Dr Schwarzstein began. 'The good news is that Lionel *is* lacking a growth hormone and we can give him injections to help him grow.'

'And the bad news?' Lionel's mum asked. She had a feeling that it would be about money.

'The bad news is that the treatment is very expensive,' the doctor explained. 'Lionel will need to have these injections every day.'

'But if I take them, will I grow?' Lionel asked. All he cared about was becoming a footballing superstar.

Dr Schwarzstein nodded. 'You'll be taller than Maradona!'

That was more than good enough for Lionel. Every

night, he gave himself the growth hormone injection – seven days in his left leg and then seven days in his right leg. It wasn't painful but it wasn't fun either. 'It will all be worth it,' he kept telling himself.

But the Messi family could only afford the first payment and so Jorge went to speak to Lionel's coach at Newell's, Adrián Coria.

'You know how much I believe in Leo's talent,' Adrián told him. Lionel was eleven years old but he still looked like he was about eight. His size was the only thing stopping him from becoming an amazing player. 'Let me speak to my bosses and see if we can give you the money. I'm sure it would be a great investment for the future of this club.'

Newell's agreed to pay for the treatment but a few months later, Jorge had only received a small amount of money. It wasn't enough and every time he asked for more, the club took a long time to reply.

'Our family can't afford to wait for each penny they give us,' he told Adrián. 'If Newell's don't care about Lionel then we'll just have to take him to another club!'

The Newell's coach hated to see Lionel leave but he also understood Jorge's frustrations. How could anyone doubt the kid's talent? All he needed was a club that really believed in him.

The Messi family discussed lots of different options. Would Lionel have a better chance of success if he went to play abroad in Italy or Spain? Or perhaps another South American club might show faith in his special gift and pay for the injections?

Lionel went to Buenos Aires for a trial at top Argentinian club River Plate, the home of his hero, Pablo Aimar. As soon as the coaches saw how small he was, they left him on the bench. He only came on to the pitch with ten minutes left but it never took long for Lionel's talent to shine brightly. He wasn't nervous at all; he had a big point to prove.

'This is why you should never judge a book by its cover,' he muttered under his breath.

With his first touch, he nutmegged River's giant centre-back and ran towards goal. His shot was powerful but the keeper made a good save. The next time he got the ball, Lionel did the same skill again. The defender was furious.

On the touchline, the coaches smiled to each other – they had struck gold. 'Whose son is that?' one of them asked the group of parents watching the trial.

Jorge stepped forward. 'Lionel is my son.'

'Great, let's talk! He's exactly the kind of player that we want here at River.'

Jorge had expected this. 'I'm afraid he is currently playing for Newell's but we would be happy to sit down and discuss a transfer.'

The River youth coaches did their best to sign Lionel. They passed on reports full of praise but the club didn't want to pay for him and his treatment.

'There are lots of talented young players that come to us,' the directors decided. 'And we don't pay special fees for them. If we lose one youngster, it's no big deal. There will be more.'

'There won't be more as good as this kid – you're saying no to the next Maradona!' the coaches warned but no-one listened.

Lionel was very disappointed when he heard the

news but his dad told him not to give up.

'When Newell's find out that River wanted to sign you, maybe they will try harder to keep you,' Jorge said, and then a smile broke out across his face. 'Plus, I think there might be an even better option than River!'

Lionel's performance at the trial had attracted other attention. Jorge had a telephone number for Josep María Minguella, a football agent who was closely linked to one of the biggest clubs in the world – Barcelona.

CHAPTER 9

THE BARCA DEAL

'Is that him?' the Barcelona technical director Charly Rexach asked, pointing at a small boy playing just behind the striker who never stopped moving.

'Yes, that's Lionel Messi,' the youth coach explained.

'Apparently that's "The New Maradona", you know!' Rexach laughed. 'He's tiny! I hope Josep is right about this kid.'

Rexach trusted Minguella's judgment; after all, he was the one who had told Barcelona to sign Maradona nearly twenty years earlier. He definitely knew what he was talking about.

Lionel was very excited about his big Spanish adventure. There were so many new experiences –

flying in a plane, leaving Argentina, going to Europe, staying in a fancy hotel. As he walked around the city of Barcelona, there was always a look of amazement on his face.

'We have McDonald's back in Argentina, you know!' his dad joked.

Lionel looked very calm about his trial but Jorge was worried. It was a massive opportunity for his son and he knew that he would be brilliant. But would his size be a problem yet again?

On his first night in Spain, Lionel was too excited to sleep. What would the training sessions be like at a top club? Would the other kids be a lot better than him? He knew he was good but was he good enough for Barcelona?

'Hi, I'm Cesc Fàbregas and I play in midfield,' a boy with black hair said in the changing room before practice. 'What's your name?'

'Lionel Messi,' he replied shyly.

'Nice to meet you,' Cesc said. 'And this is Gerard Piqué, our star centre-back.'

Gerard was very tall and he looked really strong. Suddenly, Lionel felt nervous. All of the other kids had trained together for years and they had their own jokes that he didn't understand. He was a long way away from Diego, Gerardo and Lucas, and he missed them.

'Focus!' he told himself. This was his big chance to impress.

As soon as Lionel was out on the pitch, he felt much better. With a ball at his feet, he could be anywhere in the world; it didn't matter. The session started with *rondos*, just like back in Argentina. Lionel loved *rondos*.

'Excellent!' the coaches shouted.

They played a seven-a-side game at the end, just like the 'baby' football that Lionel used to play in Argentina. It was perfect for him. With his incredible ball skills, he could always escape from defenders even in very small spaces, and he created lots of chances for his team. It was only his first day but already he was running the show. Everyone was very impressed with his performance.

'Wow, you're a nightmare to play against!' Gerard

told Lionel as they walked back to the changing room. 'I thought you'd be weak because you're so small but it's impossible to get rid of you.'

Lionel smiled. 'That's why everyone back in Argentina calls me "The Flea". They say I'm a constant menace!'

'I like that – we'll call you "The Flea" from now on!' Cesc said. 'So have you already signed for us?'

Lionel shook his head. 'Not yet.'

'Well, I hope you do – we need you!'

Rexach was away in Australia for the first week of the trial. The youth coaches asked Lionel to stay for a second week, so that the technical director could watch him in action.

'You need to see this kid!' they told him. 'We've never seen anyone that good at this age.'

Rexach walked slowly around the pitch, keeping a close eye on Lionel's movement. Every time he got the ball, he turned and attacked at speed, gliding past defenders like they weren't even there. His footwork was incredible.

'He makes everyone else look so average!' Rexach

said to himself.

Ten minutes later, he went back to the youth coaches and said, 'You're right – we have to sign him immediately!'

Unfortunately, it wasn't quite that simple to sign a thirteen-year-old boy from Argentina. Rexach was determined, but other people at the club thought it was an expensive risk.

'Charly, are you sure he's worth it?' asked the Barcelona president, Joan Gaspart. He's only a kid!'

'Yes, he's worth it, I promise,' was always Rexach's reply. 'He'll be the future of this club.'

Lionel stayed in the city, waiting to sign a contract, but two months passed and he was still not a Barcelona player.

'This is ridiculous!' Jorge told Minguella. 'Are they just wasting our time?'

Minguella met Rexach for lunch to find out what was happening, and warned him, 'Lionel can't wait forever! There are other clubs that are interested in signing him.'

No, Rexach couldn't let Lionel go elsewhere. He

took out his pen and began writing a contract on his napkin. When he finished, he gave it to Minguella. 'Look, we're serious!'

It would need to be typed up on proper paper but Lionel finally had his deal. It was a huge leap towards achieving his new dream – becoming the best player in the world.

'I can't believe it!' he told his dad as they celebrated the news. 'I'm going to play for Barcelona!'

Jorge laughed. 'I know, it's crazy, isn't it?! But don't worry – we'll be here with you every step of the way.'

The club had agreed to let Lionel live with his family in the city, rather than at the academy with the other boys. That way, he would hopefully cope better with living in a new country. Jorge and Lionel went back to Argentina to pack up their belongings.

As the Messis left their home in La Bajada, neighbours came out into the street to say goodbye. Everyone was in tears.

'We'll miss you all!'

'Good luck Leo – do us proud!'

CHAPTER 10

DIFFICULT EARLY DAYS

'How was training today?' Lionel's mother Celia asked as he came through the front door. She was worried about her son – he had always been a boy of few words but since the move to Barcelona, he had hardly said a word.

'Fine,' Lionel mumbled. He dumped his kitbag in the hallway and then disappeared into his bedroom.

Adapting to a new life was difficult for all of them. They lived in a lovely flat near the club's Nou Camp stadium with lots of bedrooms and a beautiful balcony but they missed Argentina and their friends and family.

Celia asked Jorge to speak to Lionel. He knocked on his son's door and entered.

'These first few months will be really hard,' Jorge told him, sitting down on the bed next to him. 'But if you're having any problems, please talk to us. We're here to help you.'

Lionel nodded and then after a few seconds of silence, he began: 'I just feel like such an outsider all the time. I don't fit in at all.'

'Are the other boys mean to you?' Jorge asked.

Lionel shook his head. 'No, they're nice but they all speak Catalan to each other and I don't understand a word! I hardly ever get the ball because I'm the new kid.'

'What do the coaches say?'

'They just keep talking about "the Barcelona way". They want me to do two-touch passing like everyone else but that's not my style! I like dribbling with the ball and beating defenders with my speed and skill.'

'Yes, that's what you're so good at,' Jorge said. He couldn't understand why the club would want to change the way his son played. He was a natural genius!

Lionel sighed. 'It doesn't matter. I can't play in any

official matches at the moment anyway because I'm not Spanish.'

Jorge put an arm around his son's shoulder. 'Don't give up! You'll be able to play soon and then you'll forget all about these difficult early days.'

Lionel hoped that his dad was right. For the first time, he felt like his career was going nowhere. With the hormone injections, he was getting taller but he was still under five foot, and the *Infantiles A* coach, Rodolfo Borrell, was always trying to protect him.

'Cesc, be careful with Leo!'

'Gerard, don't be so rough!'

Lionel didn't want special treatment. In Argentina, he was used to looking after himself. If defenders fouled him to win the ball, that was what referees were for. As soon as he could play official matches, he would show everyone that he was tougher than he looked.

'Leo, I've got good news! We've finally got permission for you to play,' Borrell told him one day after training.

Lionel smiled for the first time in weeks but it quickly turned to a frown.

'We want you to get lots of game time now,' his coach continued. '*Infantiles A* have a very good, settled squad, so I've decided to move you to *Infantiles B* for now.'

Throughout his childhood, Lionel had always been the tiny boy playing with much older kids. He still looked very young but for the first time, he was now the oldest player in his team.

'As long as I get to play every minute of every match, I don't care!' he told his dad.

Xavi Llorens was the coach of *Infantiles B*. After five minutes of watching Lionel in training, he was shocked.

'Why isn't he playing in the A team?' he thought to himself. 'There's no way that they have eleven players who are better than him. He's a little Maradona!'

Lionel's new teammates were shocked too – he was the best player they had ever seen.

'Coach, will Leo be playing for us all season?' they asked. 'With him in our team, we could win the league!'

Llorens couldn't answer that question but he was

desperate to keep his new star player for as long as possible. Lionel made a great start in the B team and scored in his debut.

'It's so nice to see you looking happy again!' his mum said as they walked back to their flat.

Unfortunately, the good times didn't last long at all. In only his second match, Lionel tried to block a clearance, just as the defender went to kick the ball as hard as he could.

Owwwwwwww!

He fell to the floor, holding his leg in agony. He couldn't believe it – just as he was starting to enjoy his football again, he had hurt himself. Lionel hobbled off the pitch and Jorge took him to hospital.

'How long will I be out for?' Lionel asked the doctor. He was hoping the answer would be one week, or maybe two at most.

'I'm afraid you've broken your leg,' the doctor told him, showing him the X-ray. 'No football for at least two months, I'm afraid. It's very important that you rest and let it heal.'

Lionel had never had a serious injury before. He

felt restless if he didn't kick a ball for a *day*; how could he survive *two months*?

On the journey back to the flat, Lionel didn't say a word. His season was over and it felt like his whole life was over. He sat on the sofa and played Playstation for hours.

'Let's go back to La Bajada for the summer,' Celia suggested at dinner one night. She hoped that it would help to take her son's mind off football.

Back in Argentina, Lionel had plenty of time to think about his future. Did he want to go back to Spain, or he would rather move back home?

'We will do whatever you choose,' Jorge told him.

When Barcelona called him for preseason training, Lionel had to make his decision. It had been a bad first year but he wasn't a quitter. He was a brave kid with a special gift. To achieve his dreams, he would just need to work harder than ever.

'I want to go back,' Lionel told his dad. 'I want to play for Barcelona at the highest level and I'm going to make it happen.'

CHAPTER 11

BOUNCING BACK

When Lionel returned to Spain with his dad, the rest of the family stayed behind in Argentina. Lionel spoke to his mum on the phone every night but he knew that he had to stay focused on his goal – a successful season at Barcelona. And slowly, the missing pieces of the jigsaw puzzle began to fall into place.

'It's amazing how much you've grown this year!' the club doctor told him at his check-up. 'I think it's time to stop the hormone treatment. With a healthy diet, you'll be able to reach your maximum height now.'

'What will that be?' Lionel asked excitedly.

'I think you'll be about five-foot seven, five-foot eight if you're really lucky,' the doctor told him.

'Perfect!' Lionel smiled. 'Maradona is only five-foot five!'

On the football pitch, everything was looking brighter too. The new coach, Tito Vilanova, was a big fan of Lionel and he moved him from the left wing to the middle.

'I want a very strong core,' Tito told him. 'Gerard is the leader in defence, Cesc organises things in midfield and then you have a free role up front. What a team!'

Lionel's confidence returned and soon he was back to his fearless best. He dropped deep to pick up the pass and with a neat turn, he was on the attack. The ball was stuck to his left foot as he dribbled past one defender and then with a burst of speed, he dribbled past a second. The third defender slid in for the tackle but Lionel dragged the ball back just in time. Then he calmly sent the goalkeeper the wrong way.

*Gooooooooooooooooooooooooaaaaaaaaaaaaaaaaaal
lllllllllllllllllllllllllllllllll!!!!!!!!!!*

Sometimes his teammates just stood and admired his skills.

'You always go to the left and defenders know that,' Cesc said. 'And yet, they can't get anywhere near you – I don't understand it!'

Lionel could do things that no-one else could. He was a magician – and a mystery.

'You've been here for over a year now and I know nothing about you!' Gerard admitted to him in the changing room after a victory. 'Every time we ask you to hang out with us, you say no and go home. Don't you like us?'

'No, I do! Sorry, I'm just quiet,' Lionel told him, but Gerard didn't give up.

'We're a team and I'm going to make sure that you're one of us!'

Gerard loved practical jokes and he started by hiding Lionel's towel when he went into the shower after training.

'Hey – give it back!' Lionel shouted out, but the

only response was the laughter of his teammates. In the end, he had no choice but to walk out in his pants and they all cheered.

'Looking good, Leo!' Cesc called out.

When the team stayed in a hotel for an away match, Gerard and Cesc decided to steal everything from Lionel's room. They would soon find out if he had a sense of humour or not.

'Guys, have you checked your rooms?' Lionel asked frantically as he rushed into the lounge. 'All my stuff is gone!'

His teammates pretended to be worried and followed him to his room to check. As he turned around, he saw that Gerard was filming him on his phone with a big smile on his face. He had fallen for another prank.

'I hate you guys!' Lionel shouted, but he was laughing too. It was nice to feel part of the team.

At breakfast the next morning, Gerard went to get a spoon and Lionel saw his chance. He quickly poured salt on his teammate's cereal and waited for the reaction.

Gerard took one mouthful and spat it out. 'Urghhhh!' he shouted. 'Who did that?'

Lionel and Cesc fell to the floor laughing.

The defender smiled. 'Good trick, mate. The real Leo – it's nice to finally meet you!'

After that, Lionel started to spend more and more time with his teammates. He wasn't loud and confident like Cesc and Gerard but he felt comfortable now and he loved playing in the Playstation competitions.

'Okay, so if all six of us put in five then the winner will make twenty-five profit,' Gerard suggested as they crowded round a screen in a hotel room. Everyone agreed. 'Have you played FIFA before, Leo?'

Lionel nodded but he didn't tell them the truth; he spent hours at home every day playing FIFA. He wanted to surprise them.

Three hours later, Lionel had the money in his hands.

'Is there anything you can't do?' Cesc moaned as he went off to bed.

Now that Lionel was the team's key weapon, they had to protect him even more. If opponents kicked him, Gerard often ran the full length of the pitch to have a word.

'You can't just kick him because you can't stop him,' Gerard said, towering over them. 'If you do that again, you'll have me to deal with!'

Lionel never missed a match but sometimes he was substituted if the match was already won. He hated to miss a single minute of football.

'Why did you take me off?' Lionel asked as he left the pitch. He thought he had been playing well.

The Barcelona *Juveniles A* coach, Alex Garcia, laughed. 'Because if those defenders foul you any more, you won't be able to walk tomorrow!'

At fifteen years old, Lionel was training as hard as the professionals. He was determined to keep improving and so he focused on his weaknesses. He was a decent height now but he needed to build up his strength and stamina.

'At the moment, my legs feel heavy early in the second half,' Lionel told the trainer in the gym. 'I want to be able to sprint really fast even in the last seconds of the match!'

The team won match after match, and the talented youngsters started to talk seriously about playing first-team football for Barcelona.

'They need us now!' Gerard argued. 'Luís Figo has gone to our rivals Real Madrid and at this rate, we won't even be in the Champions League next year.'

Cesc nodded but he didn't look excited. 'There's no chance of me playing in the midfield ahead of Xavi and Andrés Iniesta. They're amazing!'

Soon, Cesc was on his way to Arsenal and Gerard went to Manchester United a year later. They were big losses but Lionel decided to stay at Barcelona. He knew how close he was to becoming a superstar at the Nou Camp.

'I'll miss you,' he said to each of them as they left. 'Promise me one thing: when I make this club great again, you'll come back!'

They both nodded; that sounded really fun.

CHAPTER 12

BRIGHT START

Lionel was making very quick progress through the club ranks – first *Juveniles B*, then *Juveniles A*, then Barcelona C, and now he was training with the Barcelona B team too.

In November 2003, Barcelona arranged a friendly against Portuguese team Porto but all of their star players were away on international duty. So manager Frank Rijkaard asked the B team coach Pere Gratacós to recommend his best youth players.

'They're all brilliant, of course!' Gratacós replied but Lionel's name was at the top of the list that he gave to Rijkaard.

One evening, the phone rang in their flat. Jorge

answered it and as the call went on, the smile on his face grew bigger and bigger.

'Who was that?' Lionel asked when it was over.

'That was Josep Colomer, the Barcelona youth director,' his dad said. He was shaking with excitement. 'Son, are you ready for some great news?'

Lionel nodded eagerly and put the TV on mute.

'You're in the squad for the game in Porto!' Jorge told him.

Lionel played for so many different teams that he sometimes got confused. 'Great! For the B team, right?'

His dad shook his head. 'No, for the first team!'

Lionel couldn't believe it – he'd just received the best news ever and he was only sixteen! He barely slept at all that night because his head was full of amazing thoughts. What if he came on and scored? Would the first-team players give him advice and congratulate him if he played well? He was very nervous as he arrived at the airport with the other youth players.

'Welcome, lads!' the Barcelona captain Luis Enrique called out. 'Here's your first job!' he added, pointing to a big pile of kitbags.

Behind Enrique were Xavi and the Mexican defender Rafael Márquez. Lionel was speechless. He was standing right next to his heroes and it wasn't a dream.

Lionel was named as a substitute for the match and he waited impatiently for his chance. How long would he get – ten minutes, or more?

'Start warming up,' Rijkaard said to him with twenty minutes left.

Lionel was out of his seat in a flash, doing stretches along the side of the pitch. He took long, deep breaths but his heartbeat didn't get any slower. He couldn't wait to play football. He even had the Number 14 shirt that Barcelona legend Johan Cruyff had worn. It was time to shine, and Barcelona's new star looked calm as he ran onto the field.

'Come on, son!' Jorge cheered in the crowd. Celia and Rodrigo were also there for Lionel's big debut. They all had tears in their eyes.

With his shaggy hair flopping in front of his face, Lionel used his skill to escape from a Porto defender but he was fouled. He got back up and carried on looking for the space to create some magic. The Flea was determined to cause problems for Porto. The next couple of times, they tackled him fairly but Lionel didn't stop running, or stop dribbling with the ball. He could have scored a hat-trick.

'Wow, that kid's great!' the first-team players said to each other as they watched from the bench.

Rijkaard was impressed too. 'He's got a lot of talent and a bright future ahead of him,' the manager told the media.

Lionel was over the moon but he didn't get carried away. His debut had been a great experience but he had a long way to go before he became a first-team regular. When he returned to training with the Barcelona B team, he was more motivated than ever.

'You're like a charging bull today, Leo!' Gratacós said. 'What's got into you?'

The answer was obvious: the Porto match.

Soon Lionel was playing matches for Barcelona B

and training with the first team once a week. He was the youngest and the smallest player but he didn't worry about being out of his depth. He was in the best possible place to challenge himself and learn new things.

'Okay, now your turn,' Ronaldinho said, flicking the ball to him from behind his head.

Lionel had been welcomed into Barcelona's group of Brazilian players: Ronaldinho, Deco, Edmílson and Sylvinho. Sylvinho was the sensible one who gave him fatherly advice, and Ronaldinho was the joker who entertained him with incredible new tricks. He loved to test Lionel's technique.

'Mark my words: Leo will be better than me!' the superstar told his teammates after Lionel's very first training session.

Lionel stood there doing keepy-uppies, switching the ball from his toes to his heel, to his knee, to his chest and then to his head.

'Come on, do something special!' Ronaldinho urged him. Keepy-uppies were boring.

As the Brazilian ran in to get the ball off him,

Lionel flicked it over Ronaldinho's head, controlled it perfectly on the other side and carried on with his keepy-uppies.

'Fine, that's pretty special!' Ronaldinho admitted.

As Lionel got better and better, the first-team players kept asking Rijkaard to call him up to the squad. Finally, nearly a year after Lionel's debut against Porto, the Barcelona manager decided that he was ready.

'At first, you won't play many minutes,' Rijkaard warned him as he gave him the Number 30 shirt. 'But it's time to see what you're made of at the highest level.'

When he came off the bench against Espanyol in La Liga, Lionel became the club's youngest ever player in an official competition. It was a great achievement but that didn't interest him. He just wanted more games, and goals.

'Once I score, I'll feel much better!' Lionel told his dad.

Against Albacete, he came on with seven minutes to go. As Ronaldinho ran down the right wing, Lionel was in lots of space on the left. He called for the ball and the Brazilian delivered a great pass. Lionel controlled it perfectly, waited for the goalkeeper to dive and then chipped the ball into the other corner of the net. What a goal…

…But no – the offside flag was up.

'Next time,' Lionel said to himself as he ran back to tackle.

With two minutes to go, Ronaldinho chipped the ball over the defence again. Lionel was onside this time. As the keeper ran out of his goal, he used his side foot to lift his shot just over his outstretched arm.

Gooooooooooooooooooaaaaaaaaaaaaaaaaaaaalllllllll llllllllllllllllllllll!!!!!!!!!!!!!!!

The Nou Camp crowd roared and Lionel ran to the fans to celebrate with them. It was the best moment of his life. Ronaldinho hugged him and then lifted Lionel up on to his back. A new Barcelona star was born.

CHAPTER 13

AN AMAZING SUMMER

'Welcome to Spain!' Lionel said, giving Pablo Zabaleta a big hug. 'It's nice to see another friendly, Argentinian face around here.'

Pablo was the captain of the Under-20 national team and he had just signed for Barcelona's local rivals, Espanyol. To celebrate, Lionel had booked a table at his favourite Argentinian restaurant in the city.

'Thanks, it's been an amazing summer, hasn't it?!' Pablo laughed.

Lionel nodded and smiled. In June 2005, they had travelled to Holland together as part of the Argentina squad for the FIFA Under-20 World Cup. Lionel was one of the youngest members and he was also one of the only players who didn't play club football back in Argentina.

'It's like when I started at Barcelona,' he told his dad. 'They all know each other really well and I'm the outsider.'

'Once they see you play, you'll be one of the lads!' Jorge reassured him.

Luckily, there was one other seventeen-year-old wonderkid in the team: Sergio Agüero, the youngest player in the history of the Argentinian league. Lionel would never forget the day that he first met Sergio at a training camp. As a youngster playing at Barcelona, Lionel was already famous back home but Sergio didn't recognise him at all.

'Lionel...?' he said, asking for his surname.

'Lionel Messi,' he replied.

Suddenly, Sergio remembered the name. 'Oh, you're the guy at Barcelona!'

From that day, they became very good friends. In Holland, they shared a room and played Playstation until the coaches made them go to bed. Despite being the babies of the group, they were both hoping to play lots of games in the tournament.

'We've got a really good team,' Lionel said on the night before their first match. 'I just hope they don't think we're too young to be the stars!'

Against the USA, Lionel didn't come on until the second half and Argentina lost 1-0. After the game, Pablo went to speak to their manager, Pancho Ferraro.

'Coach, Leo has to play from the start against Egypt – we need him!'

As Argentina worked the ball down the right wing, Lionel burst through the middle. When the cross came in, the defender slipped and Lionel was in the right place to tap the ball into the net.

Goooooooooooooooooooaaaaaaaaaaaaaaaaaaaaaalllll lllllllllllllllllllllllll!!!!!!!!!!!!!!!!!!

Lionel was off the mark and it was the best feeling ever. He ran towards the fans to celebrate but then he turned to wait for his teammates. Without them, he couldn't do anything.

'If you hadn't scored today, Pancho would have blamed me!' Pablo joked.

When Colombia took a shock lead in their second-round tie, Lionel came alive again. He intercepted a pass near the halfway line and dribbled forward. He passed inside to Neri Cardozo and ran into the penalty area for the one-two. A defender slid in but Lionel dribbled round him and drilled his shot past the keeper.

Goooooooooooooooooooooooaaaaaaaaaaaaaaaalllll llllllllllllllllllllllllllllll!!!!!!!!!!!!!!

The whole team celebrated together in a big huddle. They hadn't given up and, in the last minute of the match, they scored a winner.

'Leo, do you know who we're playing next?' Pablo asked with a grin. 'Spain!'

It was nice to see Cesc again but Lionel was focused on victory. Spain were the favourites to win and that spurred Argentina on. Pablo scored first and Lionel set up a second for Gustavo Oberman. Two minutes later, a clearance fell to Lionel as he burst into the box. He brought the ball down with his right foot, then took it round the defender with his left foot and placed his shot into the corner of the net.

*Goooooooooooooooooooooaaaaaaaaaaaaaaaaaaaaallll
lllllllllllllllllllllllll!!!!!!!!!!!!!!!!!*

'That was magical!' Pablo shouted, jumping up onto Lionel's back.

Before the semi-final with Brazil, Barcelona had a special eighteenth birthday present for Lionel – a big new contract. He was playing brilliantly on the world stage and there was no way that the club were going to lose him.

'I can't stay long,' he told them as he signed. 'I've got a World Cup to win!'

Lionel got the ball on the right wing, about thirty yards from goal. He dribbled across goal with three defenders trailing behind him. As one went in for the tackle, Lionel decided to shoot. The Brazil keeper expected him to aim for the far post but instead he curled it in at the near post.

*Goooooooooooooooooooooaaaaaaaaaaaaaaaaaaaaallll
lllllllllllllllllllllllll!!!!!!!!!!!!!!!!!*

'That's even better than your goal against Spain!' Gustavo shouted.

Lionel was having the time of his life. In the last

minute of the match, he crossed for Pablo to score the winner.

As the Argentina players rested ahead of the final against Nigeria, Ferraro came to find Lionel.

'I've got someone on the phone who wants to talk to you,' the coach told him.

Lionel assumed it was a member of his family but he was in for a big surprise.

'Leo, this is Diego Maradona.'

He froze; was Sergio playing another trick on him? Was Argentina's greatest ever player really speaking to him?

'I just wanted to wish you luck – you're going to be a star. Bring home the cup!' Maradona told him.

For a second, Lionel was too overwhelmed to say anything. 'Thank you!' he managed eventually – it was a moment that he would remember forever.

Near the end of the first half, Lionel dribbled with the ball in the penalty area, waiting for teammates to join him. Suddenly, the Nigerian defender kicked him to the floor. Penalty! Lionel got up and coolly sent the keeper the wrong way. 1-0!

But Nigeria equalised and Argentina needed more magic. Sergio came on to partner Lionel in attack.

'Let's do this!' Lionel cheered.

Soon, Sergio got the ball on the right and dribbled into the box. He dummied to go left but went right and the confused defender made a clumsy foul. Another penalty!

'Great work!' Lionel said, giving him a high-five. He scored again, to make it 2-1.

When the final whistle sounded, Argentina were World Champions. As Pablo lifted the trophy, blue and white confetti filled the air. The singing and dancing went on for hours.

Lionel won three awards: the winner's medal, the Player of the Tournament, and the Top Goalscorer. The media couldn't stop talking about 'the Messi Show'. But it was a real team effort and Lionel was already looking ahead.

'This is just the start!' he said, with one arm around Pablo and the other around Sergio. 'Next, we have to win the real World Cup!'

Lionel only had to wait six weeks for his first call-up to the senior Argentina squad. Everything was happening so fast. He didn't expect to play in the friendly against Hungary but in the second half, the coach José Pékerman told him to get ready. He was about to become a full international footballer.

Wearing the Number 18 shirt, Lionel ran onto the pitch. He was determined to make an impact and so when he got the ball, he attacked at speed. He was too quick for the Hungary defender, who kicked him and pulled him back. When he tried to escape, his arm struck the defender in the face. The referee showed a yellow card to the defender and a red card to Lionel.

'No way, it was an accident!' his Argentinian teammates argued but it was no use. Lionel had been sent off on his debut. It was definitely the worst moment of his career so far.

When the players came into the changing room after the match, they found Lionel sitting alone. He was wiping away the tears with his shirt.

'Don't worry, mate!' Hernán Crespo said, trying to comfort him. 'That was never a red card.'

Gabriel Heinze tried to cheer him up. 'And you did well – for the two minutes that you were on the pitch!'

Everyone laughed and soon Lionel was feeling a bit better about it. He would get lots more chances to prove himself for Argentina. It was time to prove himself for Barcelona. Could he carry on his great form?

The answer was yes. Lionel was selected to play against Juventus in the preseason Joan Gamper tournament. There were so many superstars on the pitch – Ronaldinho, Deco, Alessandro Del Piero, Zlatan Ibrahimović – but it was an eighteen-year-old Argentinian who shone the most brightly.

Lionel twisted and turned past defenders again and again. If he lost it, he chased around until he won it back. The Flea was a constant menace. When the Juventus players couldn't stop him, they fouled him but Lionel never complained.

'He's tougher than he looks!' Rijkaard said to his coaches on the touchline.

The Barcelona fans loved his energy and his

dazzling footwork. They cheered every time Lionel got the ball. His perfect through-ball set up their first goal and he was a constant danger for the Italians.

'I have never seen a player of such quality,' the Juventus manager Fabio Capello said after the game.

In just three incredible months, Lionel had introduced himself to the football world.

In the restaurant in Barcelona, Pablo and Lionel had stopped looking back at their amazing summer. Now, Lionel was looking ahead.

'I can't wait for the new season to start!' he said.

CHAPTER 14

"THE NEW MARADONA"

After that amazing summer of 2005, Lionel's progress slowed down a bit. He struggled with leg injuries and Barcelona didn't want to rush their prodigy. They didn't need to; with Ronaldinho at his best, they were winning everything anyway.

'Do you think I'll be fit for the Champions League final?' Lionel asked Juanjo Brau, his personal trainer. Barcelona were up against Arsenal and he was desperate to play in such a major match.

'The muscle is still repairing itself,' Juanjo explained. 'It's up to Rijkaard but you might make things worse if you hurry back too soon.'

In the week before the 2006 final, Lionel trained

well and he felt fit enough to be a substitute. But unfortunately it wasn't his decision to make.

'I'm sorry but we haven't put you in the squad,' Rijkaard told him. 'You'll play in lots more finals but you're just not ready for this one.'

Lionel was furious. After months of hard work to get himself ready, he would have to watch the final from the stands instead. It was a nightmare.

When Barcelona won, Lionel didn't join them on the pitch to collect his medal, or hold the trophy. Sylvinho went looking for him and found him sitting in the dressing room.

'Come and celebrate with us! You played a big part in our success,' the Brazilian said but Lionel shook his head. He wasn't in the mood to celebrate.

But eventually, Ronaldinho and Deco brought the trophy to him in the dressing room, and once he saw Ronaldinho's infectious smile, it was impossible to feel upset for long.

'Congratulations, guys!' Lionel said, laughing. 'Next time, I'll be there in the final to help!'

After winning the Champions League, some of

his teammates lost their hunger for success. But as Ronaldinho and Deco began to fade, Lionel only got better and better. By the time Barcelona faced Real Madrid in *El Clásico* in March 2007, they were relying on their young superstar to shine.

Samuel Eto'o got the ball and looked up. It was crowded in the middle but Lionel was in space on the right. Lionel controlled the pass perfectly and beat the keeper.

Goooooooooooaaaaaaaaaaaaaallllllllllllllllllll!!!!!!!!!!

One-all! Samuel lifted him high into the air. Lionel wasn't the '*next* big thing' anymore; he was the big thing *now*. At nineteen years old, he was ready to be a star. Fifteen minutes later, he smashed the ball into the net to make it 2-2.

Unfortunately, by injury time, Real were winning 3-2. A defeat now would be a disaster for Barcelona, especially against their bitter rivals.

When Ronaldinho passed to him in the middle, Lionel didn't use his first touch to control the ball. There wasn't enough time. Instead, he used his first touch to take him in between three defenders. He was always thinking one step ahead. The Nou Camp crowd were up on their feet – could Lionel really rescue them for a third time in the game?

As he ran into the penalty area at speed, he danced around the last defender and struck his shot into the bottom corner.

Goooooooooooooooooooooooaaaaaaaaaaaaaaaaaaaaall!!!

What a time to score his first ever hat-trick! The 90,000 Barcelona fans in the Nou Camp went wild.

'How on earth did you manage that?!' Sylvinho asked as they hugged each other.

Lionel shrugged; he was just playing his natural game.

'You really *are* the new Maradona!'

For years, people had been comparing Lionel to Argentina's greatest player of all time. There were certainly similarities; they were both small, incredibly skilful playmakers and Maradona had played for Barcelona too.

'It's a real honour but it's also a lot of pressure!' Lionel admitted to his dad. He could handle the pressure, though.

In the semi-finals of the Spanish Cup against Getafe, Lionel had already set up Barcelona's first goal when he got the ball on the right, just inside his own half. Two defenders rushed to close him down but he shrugged off one and then nutmegged the other. The fans loved it.

Olé! Olé!

Two more defenders were waiting for Lionel on the edge of the penalty area. But as he dribbled forward at speed, they backed away in fear. He dribbled round one and then the other with ease. The other Barcelona players had stopped to watch the magic. Instead of shooting, Lionel dribbled round the goalkeeper too!

Goooooooooooooooooooooooooaaaaaaaaaaaaaaaaaal IIIIIIIIIIIIIIIIIIIIIIIIIIIIIIIIIIIIIIIIIIIIIIIIIIIIIIIIIIIIIIIIIIIIIIIIIIIIIIIIIIIIIIIIIIIIIIIIIIIIIIIIIIII!!!!!!!!!!!!

'If Maradona's goal against England was "Goal of the Twentieth Century", then that's definitely "Goal of the Twenty-First Century"!' Deco cheered as he jumped on Messi.

On the sidelines, Rijkaard smiled. In the crowd, both sets of supporters clapped. It was a goal that no-one would ever forget.

A few weeks later, Barcelona were losing 1-0 to local rivals, Espanyol. As the ball came into the box, Lionel jumped into the air and stretched his neck as far as it would go. He failed to head the ball; instead it hit his arm and went into the net.

Goooooooooooaaaaaaaaaaaallllllllllllllllllllll!!!!!!!!!!!!!!

As the Barcelona players celebrated, the Espanyol players ran to the referee.

'Handball!' they shouted again and again.

It wasn't Lionel's proudest moment but he always played to win.

'Were you just trying to copy Maradona again?' Xavi joked. Maradona's 'Hand of God' against England was one of the most famous goals ever.

In May 2007, Barcelona finished second in La Liga behind Real Madrid. The following year, they finished third, eighteen points away from Real Madrid. They were falling behind. It was time for a change at the club but who would come and who would go? One thing was sure – Lionel wasn't going anywhere. 'The New Maradona' was the future of Barcelona.

CHAPTER 15

OLYMPIC GOLD

'I'm afraid that Ronaldinho won't be at Barcelona next season,' club president Joan Laporta told Lionel at his home during the summer of 2008. 'I know that you two are very close and so I wanted to come here and tell you face to face.'

Lionel was sad. He would miss his mischievous Brazilian friend, but he wasn't surprised. The new Barcelona manager Pep Guardiola had decided to make some big changes, and it was time for a fresh start.

'We believe it's time for you to become our superstar,' Laporta continued. 'We want you to take the Number 10 shirt now.'

Lionel nodded – he was ready for the biggest challenge of his life.

But Barcelona was suddenly a lonely place for him; Ronaldinho had gone to AC Milan, Deco had gone to Chelsea, and Pablo had signed for Manchester City. Luckily, one familiar face returned to the club: Gerard Piqué.

'Guardiola said that you needed some protection, so I thought I better come back!' the big defender joked as they hugged.

During preseason, the new Barcelona manager could see that Lionel wasn't happy. He was scoring goals for fun but he always walked around with his head down and he barely said a word in training. Was he upset about his best friends moving away? Or was it something else? Guardiola had to find out.

'What's wrong?' he asked.

At first, Lionel stayed quiet but eventually he opened up: 'I really want to play for Argentina at the Olympics in Beijing next month but the club won't let me go.'

August was the key month to prepare his squad for

the new season but Guardiola needed his superstar to be happy. 'Let me see what I can do,' he told Lionel.

Guardiola spoke to Laporta and eventually Barcelona let Lionel go to the Olympics.

'Enjoy yourself and win the gold medal,' Guardiola told him. 'Then come back here and win lots more trophies!'

Lionel smiled for the first time in weeks. 'Thanks, I will!'

He couldn't wait for the tournament to begin. With Pablo in defence, Javier Mascherano, Ángel Di Maria and Juan Román Riquelme in midfield, and Lionel and Sergio Agüero in attack, Argentina were the favourites.

'If we don't win gold, we won't be allowed to return home!' Sergio said and everyone laughed.

In the first match against the Ivory Coast, Lionel scored Argentina's first goal and set up the second. He was enjoying himself, just like Guardiola had told him to. With two more wins, they qualified for the quarter-finals.

'Holland will be our toughest opponents so far,'

the captain Juan Román told his teammates before kick-off. 'We'll need to play really well today!'

After ten minutes, Lionel blocked a clearance and sprinted towards goal. Two defenders chased after him but he calmly chested the ball down, dribbled around the goalkeeper and smashed it into the back of the net.

Gooooooooooooooooooooooaaaaaaaaaaaaaaaaalllll lllllllllllllllllllllllll!!!!!!!!!!!!!!!!

'You made that look so easy!' Sergio shouted as they celebrated together.

But after a great start, Holland equalised and Argentina couldn't grab a second goal. In extra-time, Lionel dropped deeper, trying to create a moment of magic to win the game. He dribbled slowly towards goal, looking for a teammate to pass to. As three players surrounded him, Lionel spotted Ángel's brilliant run and played a perfect through-ball. His teammate scored to take them through to the semi-finals.

'What a tough match!' Juan Román said afterwards. 'Thank goodness we had you, Leo!'

In the semi-finals, Argentina faced Brazil, captained by Lionel's good friend Ronaldinho.

'If we don't win this, Ronnie will never let me forget it!' he said in the dressing room.

'The whole of Argentina won't let us forget it if we lose to Brazil!' Pablo reminded him.

Lionel played well but Sergio was Argentina's star, with two goals in the second half. At the final whistle, Ronaldinho looked very disappointed but he hugged Lionel.

'Good luck in the final,' the Brazilian said.

Argentina faced Nigeria in the gold medal match, just like they had at the World Youth Championships three years earlier. Could they do it again? Lionel had his heart and mind set on victory. Gold – that's what Guardiola had told him to win.

Lionel got the ball on the right and did a beautiful 'Maradona turn' past the defender. The Argentina fans in the stadium roared. He had the space to shoot but his thundering strike was saved by the keeper.

'Keep going – the goal will come!' Juan Román urged his teammates.

Lionel received the ball with his back to goal, just inside his own half. He turned neatly and spotted another one of Ángel's brilliant runs. He played the pass and Ángel was through on goal. From the edge of the penalty area, he chipped the ball over the goalkeeper's head and into the net. 1-0!

'Great pass!' Ángel said to Lionel.

'Great run!' Lionel replied. 'And great finish!'

Forty minutes later, Argentina were the winners. The players linked arms and danced around the centre-circle. Maradona was there, clapping in the crowd.

'We're national heroes now!' Sergio cheered as they did a lap of honour around the pitch.

With the Argentinian anthem playing loudly, Lionel bowed his head so that the gold medal could be placed around his neck. It was a very proud moment for him, his family and his country. He had come to the Olympics and achieved his aim.

Now it was time to return to Barcelona for his next challenges: another La Liga title and the Champions League trophy. Lionel had a lot to thank Guardiola for.

CHAPTER 16

THE TREBLE

'What was that?!' Guardiola shouted in the dressing room. He was furious because Barcelona had been beaten 1-0 by Numancia in their first league match of the 2008/09 season. It was a dreadful start. 'You were brilliant in preseason but today you forgot everything that you learned!'

Lionel stared at the floor in silence. He hated losing, but at the same time he was excited about Guardiola's new style of football. Although Lionel played on the right, with Thierry Henry on the left and Samuel Eto'o in the middle, he was now at the centre of everything, with more time on the ball and more chances to score. It would take a few weeks for the players to adapt but soon Barcelona would be unstoppable. Lionel would make sure of that.

Soon they faced Sporting Gijón. As Bojan Krkić cut inside, Xavi overlapped down the left wing. Barcelona were playing beautiful, flowing football. 'Pass and move, pass and move!' Guardiola kept telling them. Xavi crossed the ball first time and Lionel powered his header into the top corner.

Gooooooooooooooooaaaaaaaaaaaaaaalllllllllllllllllllll lllllllllllllll!!!!!!!!!!!!!!!!!!!!!

'What a great team goal!' Lionel cheered as he gave Bojan and Xavi high-fives.

The Sporting Gijón goalkeeper sat down on the grass and admitted defeat. They were losing 6-1.

By the time that Barcelona played Real Madrid in December, Lionel had already scored fourteen goals in all competitions and the club were top of La Liga.

'How are you feeling?' the club physio asked.

'Amazing!' Lionel replied with a big smile.

It was the truth. For the first time, he was enjoying an injury-free season. Guardiola had put him on a strict diet and it was really working. Lionel wasn't allowed to drink Coca-Cola or eat burgers anymore but it was worth it to feel so healthy. He felt like there was nothing that he couldn't achieve if he put his mind to it.

'Let's show Real that we're back to our best!' the captain, Carles Puyol, shouted before kick-off and the whole team roared. They were up for the big game.

Samuel scored the first goal and Lionel made it 2-0 with a glorious chip. What a moment! He took his shirt off and ran towards the bench for a massive team hug. Nothing could beat the feeling of scoring an important goal in *El Clásico*. Lionel had never heard so much noise in the Nou Camp. Barcelona were on fire and even the manager was smiling.

'Real will want revenge,' Guardiola warned ahead of the return match at the Bernabeu. His team was very close to securing the league title for the first time in three years. They just needed to stay focused.

Madrid took the lead but with Xavi, Andrés Iniesta and Lionel at their best, Barcelona soon fought back.

There was no way that Lionel was going to let the trophy slip away; not when they had all worked so hard for it. He scored twice as they won 6-2.

'We thrashed them!' Carles joked after the match. 'Even Gerard scored!'

Lionel felt on top of the world – he had twenty-three league goals with three games to go, and his team was playing amazing football. The party didn't last long, however, because Barcelona had another big game four days later: the second leg of their Champions League semi-final against Chelsea.

'I need to *play* in a European final!' Lionel told his teammates.

He still thought about the night when he watched his teammates win against Arsenal without him. That painful memory had spurred him on to great things. Lionel saved his best form for Europe, scoring crucial goals to defeat Lyon and Bayern Munich. He was now one step away from another final.

When Chelsea scored, it looked like Barcelona's Champions League dreams were over for another year. But Lionel never gave up. With seconds to go, he got the ball on the left side of the penalty area. He was tempted to shoot but there were three defenders in front of him. Lionel did the sensible thing; he passed to Andrés instead, who had just enough space to hit a brilliant strike into the top corner. 1-1!

'You did it!' Lionel screamed, jumping on his teammate. 'We've won on away goals!'

Lionel couldn't wait to end an amazing season with his first two finals for Barcelona. He knew that great players scored great goals in the biggest games. This was why he had moved all the way from Argentina to Spain when he was only thirteen years old. He was a great player and he was going to show it by winning trophies.

First up: Athletic Bilbao in the Copa del Rey, the Spanish Cup. Again, Barcelona went 1-0 down but they had the confidence to fight back. With Lionel in the team, a game was never over until the final whistle. Yaya Touré scored a great goal to make it 1-1 but could they go on to victory?

Early in the second half, Lionel dribbled past a defender and slipped a great pass to Samuel in the penalty area. His shot was saved but the ball bounced out towards the edge of the box. After the pass, The Flea had kept running. He took one touch and smashed his shot into the net.

Gooooooooooooooooooooaaaaaaaaaaaaaaaaaaaaallllllllll llllllllllllllllllll!!!!!!!!!!!!!!!!!!!!!!

Lionel ran towards the fans and slid along the grass. His dad was right; hearing thousands of people chanting your name really was the best feeling in the world.

'You did it!' Gerard shouted, jumping on top of his old friend.

Soon, Lionel could hardly breathe at the bottom of a big pile of players but he didn't mind. He was always happy to be the hero.

As the match restarted, the smile left Lionel's face. He was 100 per cent focused on winning and ten minutes later, Barcelona were 4-1 up. Could anyone stop Guardiola's team?

'It's great to win the double,' he told Xavi as they celebrated afterwards, 'but the treble would be unbelievable!'

In the Champions League final, Lionel's Barcelona faced Cristiano Ronaldo's Manchester United. The two best players in the world faced each other, as did the two best teams in the world. The football world was very excited.

'You've been brilliant all season,' Guardiola told his players before kick-off. 'We just need one more win!'

The atmosphere inside the Stadio Olimpico in Rome was unbelievable. Lionel looked calm as he listened to the Champions League anthem but inside he was buzzing. Barcelona were back on Europe's biggest stage and this time, he was playing. It didn't get any better than that.

Ronaldo made a bright start for United but Samuel gave Barcelona the lead. After the goal, the team calmed down and started playing the passing football that Guardiola had taught them. The Manchester United players ran and ran but they couldn't get the ball off Andrés and Xavi in midfield. A second goal seemed inevitable but Lionel wanted to be the one to score it.

As Xavi ran forward down the right, Lionel made his move in the box. The cross was excellent and so were Lionel's leap and header. The goalkeeper Edwin van der Sar just stood and watched as the ball flew into the far corner.

Goooooooooooooooooooaaaaaaaaaaaaaaaaaaaaaallll llllllllllllllllllllllll!!!!!!!!!!

Lionel's right boot fell off but he picked it up and kissed it like a trophy. He sank to his knees and pointed to the sky, where his grandmother Celia was always watching him. She would be so proud of him. It was a moment that Lionel would never forget. In the first battle of Messi versus Ronaldo, he was the winner. Lionel had confirmed his reputation as the best player in the world.

Back in the dressing room, Lionel and Guardiola hugged. What a spectacular season it had been.

CHAPTER 17

'FALSE NINE'/
BALLON D'OR

'There's no way you won't win the Ballon d'Or this year!' Andrés said.

'What about you, or Xavi?' Lionel replied modestly. 'You're both on the shortlist too!'

But Lionel really hoped his teammate was right. After finishing behind Cristiano Ronaldo for two years in a row, he was desperate to finish first this time. 'The best player in the world' was the title that he had wanted since he was four years old. In the 2008/09 season, he had won the treble for Barcelona, scoring thirty-eight goals – what more did he have to do?

'And the winner of the 2009 Ballon d'Or is...'

the presenter began at the ceremony in Paris. Lionel crossed his fingers under the table. '…Lionel Messi!'

The whole room clapped as he made his way to the stage. Lionel looked at the massive golden trophy and smiled. When it was handed to him, his smile grew even bigger. It was his trophy now – he was officially the best player in the world.

The only bad thing about winning was that he had to make a speech. He felt more nervous talking in front of a crowd than he ever did on the pitch, even in the Champions League final.

'I'm really happy to win this!' Lionel said and then he thanked his family, his teammates and his manager, Pep Guardiola. He was very relieved when it was all over. Now, he could go back to what he did best and loved most: playing football.

Samuel Eto'o had been replaced by Zlatan Ibrahimović but that was the only change at Barcelona. They were still winning almost every game, and Lionel was still scoring and creating lots of goals. He was the world's most famous footballer but that had only increased his desire to win. When

Barcelona lost to Sevilla in the Copa del Rey, Lionel cried on the pitch.

Guardiola put an arm around him. 'Leo, we won six trophies out of six last year – the Spanish Super Cup, the UEFA Super Cup, La Liga, the Copa del Rey, the Champions League and even the FIFA Club World Cup. No-one has ever done that before. At some point, we had to lose!'

Lionel nodded and wiped his face but he was already thinking about ways to improve.

'Coach, I know I can play even better if I get more time on the ball,' he told Guardiola in his office a few weeks later. 'I don't want to play on the right wing anymore – I want to play through the middle as the 'False Nine' again. Do you remember how well it worked against Real Madrid last season, and in the Champions League final against Manchester United?'

Guardiola listened carefully and agreed with his superstar. 'Let me discuss it with my coaches,' he replied.

Some players complained that he gave Lionel special treatment but there was a good reason for that – Lionel *was* special. When he played as the 'False Nine' – a central striker who had the freedom to roam around the pitch – defenders didn't know what to do. If Lionel dropped deep to pick up passes from Andrés and Xavi, should they follow him and leave a gap at the back? Usually, they were cautious and that gave Lionel more space to turn and run towards goal.

'If Lionel is happy, Barcelona win,' Guardiola said to his assistant, Tito Vilanova. 'It's as simple as that!'

'Then let's make sure he's happy!' Vilanova replied.

In April 2010, Zlatan was out of action due to injury, and Lionel got his opportunity in the centre. He had two big tests ahead of him – the second leg of the Champions League quarter-final against Arsenal, and then another *El Clásico* against Real Madrid. If it went well, surely Guardiola would let him play there every week?

'We need lots of goals from you, now that you're our central striker,' his manager told Lionel.

'Don't worry – I won't let you down!' he replied.

From the very first minute against Arsenal, The

Flea was at his most dangerous. It was impossible to mark him because he never stopped moving. And every time he got the ball, he looked for a killer pass or dribbled towards goal. When Arsenal took the lead, he became even more determined. He was in the mood to score.

Lionel got the ball just outside the penalty area and tried to play a one-two with Xavi. A defender blocked it but the rebound fell to Lionel again. With his quick feet, he controlled it and curled a fierce shot into the top corner.

Goooooooooooooooooaaaaaaaaaaaaaaaaaaaaaalllllllllll llllllllllllllllllllllllll!!!!!!!!!!!!!!!!

It was a magical strike, exactly when Barcelona needed it most. The fans went wild, especially when Lionel flapped his arms up and down to say, 'You can make more noise than that!'

Just before half-time, he completed his hat-trick. As the goalkeeper rushed out to block his shot, Lionel chipped the ball perfectly over his head.

'I can't believe you just did that!' Andrés shouted, giving him a high-five.

Few players would have dared to try it but Lionel was full of confidence. He kissed the Barcelona badge on his shirt – the club meant so much to him.

The final score was 4-1 and Lionel had scored all four goals to take his team through to the semi-finals.

'Okay, you proved your point today!' Guardiola joked, giving his 'False Nine' a big hug.

'He's the best player in the world by some distance,' Arsenal manager Arsène Wenger told the media. 'He's like a PlayStation.'

Against Real Madrid at the Bernabeu, Lionel dribbled forward, passed to Xavi and then kept running into the penalty area. The defenders didn't follow him and so Xavi did what he did best: pass. Lionel controlled it with his chest and tapped the ball past the goalkeeper.

Goooooooooooooooooooooooaaaaaaaaaaaaaaaaaalllll lllllllllllllllllll!!!!!!!!!!!!!!!!!!

'There's no stopping you at the moment!' Xavi cheered, lifting Lionel into the air. The La Liga title was nearly theirs.

But Zlatan was back for the Champions League

semi-final against Inter Milan, and so Lionel returned to the right. Suddenly, the beautiful standard of football disappeared; Lionel was wasted out on the wing and Barcelona lost 3-1 on aggregate.

'From now on, Lionel plays through the middle,' Guardiola told his coaches after the match. 'He's the best player in the world!'

That was official; thanks to his forty-seven goals, Lionel won the Ballon d'Or for the second year in a row.

CHAPTER 18

MESSI VS RONALDO

'This is war!' captain Carles Puyol told his teammates.

The Barcelona–Real Madrid rivalry had always been fierce but by 2011, it was fiercer than ever. It had become a battle of the top managers – Pep Guardiola versus José Mourinho. And it had become a battle of the superstars – Messi versus Ronaldo.

In April, the two teams played each other four times: once in La Liga, once in the Copa del Rey final, and then twice in the Champions League semi-finals.

'Well, there's no better way to show that we're the best!' Lionel argued, as competitive as ever.

The league match ended in a tense 1-1 draw, which kept Barcelona eight points clear at the top. Lionel scored a penalty and then with ten minutes to go, Cristiano scored a penalty. Messi 1 Ronaldo 1.

'Anything you do, Ronaldo does too!' Andrés said with a big smile on his face. Lionel's teammates loved to tease him about his Ballon d'Or rival. They needed their star to be at his very best.

In the Copa del Rey final, Lionel was desperate to be the matchwinner. He tried dropping deep, he tried moving out to the wing but nothing worked. Wherever he went, he was surrounded by defenders. Then in extra time, Cristiano scored to give Real the victory. Messi 1 Ronaldo 2.

Lionel was furious. He always hated losing but losing against Ronaldo and Real Madrid was the worst feeling ever.

'What are we going to do?' he asked his teammates. 'We have to win the Champions League semi-final now!'

The first leg was away at the Bernabeu and Guardiola asked his players to put lots of pressure on the Real defenders. 'Tackle, tackle, tackle but don't be reckless! Remember, we're at home in the second leg.'

The Madrid fans booed Lionel every time he touched the ball. He was used to that. He never stopped running but Real were marking him out of the match.

'Something has to change!' Lionel thought. He was getting more and more frustrated with himself.

After sixty minutes, the match did change; Madrid's defender Pepe was sent off for a dangerous tackle.

'Come on, we've got to take advantage of the extra man!' Carles shouted from defence.

The Barcelona pressure was building. Xavi passed to Ibrahim Afellay on the right wing. Ibrahim dribbled into the area and looked up.

'I'm here!' Lionel called. He had made a great run in between the centre-backs and he steered the ball into the net.

Gooooooooooooooooaaaaaaaaaaaaaaaalllllllllllllllll llllllll!!!!!!!!!!!!!!!!!!!!!!!

The whole team celebrated together, including the substitutes who were warming up. It was a wonderful moment. Lionel pumped his fists at the fans and pointed to the Barcelona badge on his shirt. It was another proud day and he wasn't finished yet.

With five minutes to go, Lionel burst forward and his teammates just stood and watched 'The Messi Show'. He went past one defender and then another. The Barcelona fans were already standing in anticipation – they had seen the special things that Lionel could do with the ball at his feet.

Olé! Olé!

Lionel was in the penalty area now and so the Real defenders had to be careful not to foul him. He was too skilful for them anyway. Just when he looked like he was about to fall over, he stretched his leg out and kicked the ball into the bottom corner.

Goooooooooooooooooooooaaaaaaaaaaaaaaaaaaaaaall llllllllllllllllllllllll!!!!!!!!!!!!!

'That's one of the best goals I've ever seen!' Carles screamed in Lionel's ear.

Messi 3 Ronaldo 2.

As long as Barcelona didn't lose in the second leg at the Nou Camp, they were through to another Champions League final. The Flea worked hard for his team, closing down defenders all over the pitch.

'I didn't know you could tackle!' Gerard joked at half-time.

When Pedro scored, Lionel was one of the first players to slide across the grass and congratulate him. Football was a team effort – he couldn't succeed without brilliant players like Carles and Gerard in defence, Xavi and Andrés in midfield, and Pedro and David Villa in attack. He knew that he was very lucky to have the best teammates in the world.

In the final, Barcelona played Manchester United again but this time it was in England at Wembley.

'We beat them two years ago and we're an even better team this time,' Guardiola told his players but the spirit was already very high. They were determined to win.

It was 1-1 at half-time but Lionel didn't panic. He only needed a tiny bit of space to create magic.

He moved back alongside Andrés, Xavi and Sergio Busquets to make it four-versus-two in central midfield. When Andrés passed to him, Lionel now had a big gap in front of him. He dribbled forward and hit a powerful, swerving shot into the bottom corner.

Goooooooooooooooooaaaaaaaaaaaaaaaaaaaallllllll llllllllllllllllllll!!!!!!!!!!!!!!!!!!

Lionel ran to the Barcelona fans with his arms and legs flying all over the place. He was so happy. He had scored another very important goal in a major final.

Messi 4 Ronaldo 2.

At the final whistle, Lionel threw his arms up in the air and hugged Xavi.

'Well done, that's your third Champions League title!' Lionel shouted.

Xavi laughed. 'It's your third, too!'

'No, I don't count that first one – I didn't play.'

'We'll have to win another one, then – I know how much you love a hat-trick!'

The Manchester United manager, Sir Alex

Ferguson, came over to congratulate Lionel. 'We did our best but we just couldn't stop you today!'

Lionel thanked him for his kind words. It was a real honour to be praised by such an amazing coach.

As Guardiola walked around the pitch, he spotted Lionel. He gave him the biggest hug of all. The manager only said two words to his superstar: 'Thank you'.

It had been a very tough battle against Real Madrid but Barcelona had finished the season with two big trophies. Two out of three was a great achievement.

'Well done, son!' Jorge said as they celebrated with an end-of-season meal. 'Fifty-three goals in one season – that's incredible!'

'Yes, but do you know how many Cristiano scored?' Lionel asked his dad.

Jorge shook his head.

'Fifty-three as well!'

The race was on.

CHAPTER 19

GOALS, GOALS, GOALS

'Look who's back!' Gerard shouted in the middle of preseason training. Lionel turned around to see Cesc Fàbregas smiling and waving. It was great to have the old gang together again.

'The three of us can play Playstation in the same room now!' Lionel laughed.

With Cesc now playing alongside Andrés, Xavi and Sergio, Barcelona definitely had the best midfield in the world. Lionel was very excited. He needed clever, creative players around him to help him achieve his number one aim: goals, goals, goals.

In the Spanish Super Cup against Real Madrid, Lionel chested the ball down to Gerard, who flicked it through for the one-two. Lionel dribbled towards the goal and at the last second, he lifted the ball beautifully over the diving goalkeeper. 2-1! Barcelona were winning and Lionel was the hero yet again.

'You're going to get bored of celebrating all of my goals this year!' he told David Villa.

With five minutes to go, the score was 2-2. Lionel was determined to win his first trophy of the year, especially against Cristiano Ronaldo's Real Madrid. Cesc passed to Lionel, who passed first time to Adriano on the right wing. His cross was perfect and Lionel scored with a powerful volley.

Goooooooooooooaaaaaaaaaaaallllllllllllllllllllllll!!!!!!!!

He jumped into Cesc's arms and punched the air. What a start to the season!

By December, Lionel had already scored seventeen goals in La Liga, including two hat-tricks.

'But more importantly, how many has Cristiano scored so far?' Cesc joked on the flight to Japan for the FIFA World Club Cup. Everyone was really enjoying the rivalry.

'He's got seventeen too but Real Madrid are top

of the league,' Lionel said. 'I've scored more in the Champions League but I think he's winning at the moment!'

In the World Club Cup final, Barcelona played Brazilian team Santos. Their superstar was a skilful, young attacker called Neymar.

'Have you seen the videos of him?' Gerard asked Lionel. 'He's the real deal. One day, he might be better than you!'

'Let the battle begin!' Lionel replied with a smile. After Messi vs Ronaldo, it was now Messi vs Neymar.

Lionel passed to Cesc, who passed to Xavi, who passed back to Lionel as he burst into the box. It was Barcelona's pass-and-move football at its very best. Lionel chipped the keeper to complete a brilliant team goal.

'I bet Guardiola loved that one!' Andrés laughed as the whole team celebrated together.

In the second half, Lionel made it 4-0 by dribbling around the goalkeeper. There was a clear winner in the Messi vs Neymar battle. After the match, he went to speak to the Brazilian. He looked upset about losing the final.

'Well played today,' Lionel said. 'You should come and play with me at Barcelona – it would be fun!'

Neymar's frown turned into a smile. 'That would be amazing!'

On the flight home to Spain, Lionel was in a good mood. 'Another trophy and two more goals – that's not bad for a week's work!'

'And next week, you could win another Ballon d'Or,' Cesc reminded him.

At the FIFA ceremony in Switzerland, Lionel won his third trophy in a row. He had now won as many as legends Johan Cruyff, Michel Platini and Marco van Basten.

'It's an amazing honour,' Lionel said in his speech. 'I want to share this award with my teammate, Xavi. He finished third this year and it's such a pleasure to play with him.'

Xavi hugged and thanked Lionel but then it was back to their usual banter.

'You've come a long way, mate, especially in terms of your style!' Xavi joked. 'Have you seen the photos from a few years ago? You looked a mess with your long hair and baggy suit! Now you've got a smart haircut and a velvet jacket – is Cristiano giving you fashion advice?'

Back on the pitch, Lionel scored two against Real Betis and then a hat-trick against Málaga.

'When did you become such a goal machine?' Cesc asked with a cheeky smile. 'Was it when I returned?'

Barcelona relied on Lionel more than ever. When he felt ill ahead of their Champions League match against Bayer Leverkusen in March 2012, Guardiola was worried.

'Why don't you start on the bench?' the manager suggested. 'If you're feeling better in the second half, you can come on.'

Lionel shook his head. Missing the match would only make him feel worse. 'No, I'm fine. I just need a paracetamol and then I'll be ready to play.'

After twenty-five minutes, Lionel burst through and scored with his trademark finish: the lob.

Goooooooooooooaaaaaaaaaaaalllllllllllllllllllllllll!!!!!!!!

Lionel danced through the defence again and again with his perfect balance and lightning quick feet. It was one of those games where he was simply unstoppable. By the final whistle, he had five goals and Barcelona were 7 1 winners.

'What a masterclass!' Cesc said, giving Lionel a big hug. 'Are you still feeling ill?'

'No, I feel a lot better now!'

Two weeks later, Lionel broke a big club record. With his hat-trick against Granada, he became Barcelona's greatest ever goalscorer.

'Wow, 233 goals!' Andrés said. It was an incredible achievement. 'And you're only nineteen!'

Lionel laughed. 'Ha ha, very funny, I'm much older than that. I'm twenty-four now!'

But despite all of his goals, Barcelona struggled in the biggest games of the season. When teams man-marked Lionel, he needed players around him to create chances instead. But against Real Madrid in La Liga and Chelsea in the Champions League, the magic was missing. Lionel even missed a penalty against Chelsea.

Lionel sat silently in the dressing room, holding back his tears. 'No Spanish League title and no

European final – this is our worst season in years!' he mumbled eventually.

'Our season isn't over yet,' Guardiola reminded him. 'We've still got the Copa del Rey final to win.'

In the Copa del Rey final against Athletic Bilbao, Lionel scored the second goal as Barcelona won 3-0. He was pleased to finish the season with at least one trophy.

'So how many goals did you get in the end?' Jorge asked his son.

Lionel didn't need to do the maths, even though it was a very big number. 'I got fifty in the league and seventy-three in total.'

'And Cristiano?' his dad continued.

'He got forty-six in the league and sixty in total. It's a team game, though – this season, he won La Liga and I didn't.'

When the 2012/13 season started, Lionel carried on scoring goals. By December 2012, he had broken another record. In one single year, he had scored an unbelievable ninety-one goals for Barcelona and Argentina.

CHAPTER 20

ANTONELLA AND THIAGO

'Today I am the happiest man in the world,' Lionel wrote on his Facebook page. He had big news and he wanted everyone to know. 'My son has been born.'

Since leaving Argentina when he was thirteen years old, Lionel had returned to Rosario every summer. Every summer he met up with his old friend Lucas Scaglia and every time he made sure that he saw Lucas's cousin Antonella Roccuzzo. Lionel refused to give up on her.

'She gets more and more beautiful every time I see her,' he told Lucas. 'One day, she'll be my girlfriend.'

Lucas didn't argue. Lionel had been saying that since he was nine years old, and he had the same determined look on his face that he always had on the football pitch. It was best to stay quiet and let him work his magic.

When Antonella broke up with her boyfriend, she began spending more and more time with Lionel. It wasn't football or fame that attracted her to him; it was his kindness. When one of her friends died, Lionel flew back to Argentina to comfort her.

'Shouldn't you be playing football?' Antonella asked him.

He shrugged and held her hand. 'Don't worry – football can wait. You're more important!'

She smiled and kissed him on the cheek. 'When we were younger, I thought you were one of those stupid boys who only think and talk about football but I was wrong. You're a very sweet guy.'

Lionel had always loved Antonella but soon she fell in love with him too. He returned to Barcelona and she carried on studying in Rosario, but they were now in a relationship.

'When shall we tell people?' Antonella asked when Lionel next came to visit her. He was a very private person and he had asked her to keep everything a secret at first.

He shook his head. 'Not yet. Once they know, the newspapers won't leave us alone! Right now, I'm enjoying the calm before the storm.'

When Lionel felt comfortable, he gave the media a first clue. On a Spanish TV show in 2009, they asked him if he had a girlfriend.

He told the truth with a smile on his face. 'Yes, she lives in Argentina.'

The storm broke and a few months later, Antonella was living happily in Barcelona with Lionel. After years of chasing, another dream had finally come true.

'Amazing things come to those who wait!' Lionel joked with Lucas.

'Yes, I guess we're related now,' Lucas replied, pretending to be unhappy about that.

In June 2012, Lionel scored a great goal for Argentina against Ecuador. But it wasn't the goal that everyone was talking about; it was the goal celebration. After hugging his teammates, he picked up a football and put it under his shirt. The rumours spread immediately.

'Lionel is having a child!'

'Mrs Messi must be pregnant!'

In November 2012, Antonella gave birth to a son and they called him Thiago. Lionel was both excited and nervous about his new responsibility. At twenty-five, he had to act like a proper adult now.

'I'll have to start thinking about someone other than myself,' he admitted to Antonella. 'I will certainly have less time to play Playstation!'

Lionel's great friend Sergio Agüero gave them a tiny Argentina kit with '10 THIAGO' emblazoned on the back. Teammates new and old also sent messages.

'Congratulations, has he kicked a ball yet?' Xavi asked.

'Is Thiago signed up with the Barcelona Academy? If not, do it straight away!' Carles wrote.

'I'm honoured that you chose my name!' Thiago Motta texted.

Jorge was a very proud granddad and Lionel was

a very proud dad. On Father's Day, he got his son's name and handprint tattooed on the back of his left leg. 'Now every time I score, Thiago is part of it.'

When Lionel scored two goals against Mallorca a week later, he sucked his thumb, the classic way for footballers to celebrate the births of their children.

Soon, Thiago was watching his dad from the stands with Antonella. There was an unlimited supply of baby Barcelona shirts for him to wear.

'What happens if he's really bad at football?' Antonella asked one day at home.

'It doesn't matter,' Lionel replied. 'If he's a son of mine, he'll be excellent at something!'

CHAPTER 21

CHANGES

'Please don't leave – we need you!'

'This is your team. Without you, we would not have become the best in the world.'

At the end of the 2011/12 season, Lionel could see that Guardiola was struggling as Barcelona's manager. He looked tired and fed up. Lionel sent him text messages to try and persuade him to stay but it was no good.

'Guys, I have something to tell you,' Guardiola began when all of his players had arrived for training. 'I've decided to take a break from management. We've achieved so much over the last few years and I'm sure that you'll go on to achieve lots more in the next few years. Thank you for everything!'

It was a very sad day. Lionel couldn't believe it.
He was so grateful for everything that Guardiola had
done for him. Who could possibly take over from
Barcelona's most successful manager ever?

'Tito Vilanova will be your new manager,'
Guardiola confirmed.

Lionel was relieved – it was a very good choice.
Vilanova had been Barcelona's assistant manager
for years and so he understood their game plan. He
had even coached Lionel way back when he was
a tiny fourteen-year-old learning about the 'False
Nine' role.

Barcelona made the best start ever to a La Liga
season but just as they were flying, Vilanova fell
ill and had to take two months off to recover from
surgery.

'I hope he gets better soon,' Lionel said to Andrés.
'We need our manager back!'

At still only twenty-six, Lionel was now one of
the senior players. The other players depended on
him, especially when everything was so uncertain.

He kept scoring goals but when Xavi and Carles got injured, Barcelona looked weak without their leaders. Mourinho's Real Madrid beat them in the Copa del Rey and then in La Liga too. Their season was falling apart.

'Come on, we've got to do better than that!' Lionel screamed as he stormed into the dressing room.

It was a frustrating time for Lionel. After four years without an injury, he had pulled a muscle in his right leg. He could still play in the big games but only if he rested in between. Life on the bench was miserable but when he came on, Lionel always changed the game.

'You don't even have to touch the ball,' Andrés laughed. 'You just have to step on to the pitch and our opponents are terrified!'

Barcelona won the Spanish League title but they lost 7-0 on aggregate to Bayern Munich in the Champions League. Lionel limped through the first leg and didn't leave the bench in the second leg. It was a very embarrassing end to a difficult season for the Spanish club.

'I'm afraid my illness is getting worse,' Vilanova told his team during the summer. He didn't look well at all. 'This is my dream job but I have to leave.'

Lionel wished his manager well and wondered who would be next. He didn't like changes.

Three days later, Barcelona named their new manager – Gerardo Martino, the coach at Lionel's favourite Argentinian team, Newell's Old Boys.

'Do you know him?' Andrés asked.

'Not really but my dad does,' Lionel replied. 'He says that he's turned Newell's into a really successful and exciting team.'

And Martino wasn't the only change at Barcelona. The young Brazilian superstar Neymar had arrived for a figure said to be £48 million.

'You've got a new rival now!' Gerard joked.

Lionel shook his head and laughed. 'No, I've got a new strike partner. He's a great player. Finally, I won't have to score *all* of our goals!'

Alexis Sánchez dribbled down the right wing and crossed into the Real Sociedad penalty area. Neymar made a great run from the left wing to the six-yard box and tapped the ball into the net. 1-0! Lionel was the first player to run over and hug him.

Three minutes later, Neymar ran down the left wing and crossed into the box. It went over Alexis's head but Lionel was there at the back post to score with a diving header. 2-0!

Gooooooooooooooooooooaaaaaaaaaaaaaaaaaaaaaaa aalllllllllllllllllllllllll!!!!!!!!!!!!!!!!

Lionel got up and pointed at Neymar. 'Great assist!' he shouted as they hugged. Barcelona's new attack was looking very, very dangerous.

But just as their season got going, Lionel picked up another injury. Against Real Betis, he dribbled forward and as he stretched to play a pass to Neymar, he felt a lot of pain in his leg.

Owwwwwwwwwwwww!

As the match continued, Lionel lay on the grass in agony. Slowly, he got up and tried to carry on but he couldn't. Eventually, he stood still and waited to be substituted.

'It's a serious injury,' the physio warned Lionel after the match. 'You can't just rest for a week and then come back and play. It will take time for your leg to heal.'

It was awful news but Lionel was desperate to be fit for the 2014 World Cup in Brazil. This time, he wouldn't rush his recovery. But he couldn't just sit around and watch his teammates playing without him. He decided to go home to Argentina.

'I need to get away from Barcelona and relax for a bit,' he told Martino, who agreed.

But Lionel didn't relax for long. As soon as he could, he was working hard in the gym every day. He lost weight and felt healthier than he had for a long time.

'I'm ready for my comeback!' he told Martino excitedly.

In January 2014, after two months out of action, Lionel came off the bench for the last half-hour against Getafe in the Copa del Rey. As he ran on to the pitch, the Barcelona fans cheered loudly. It was a great feeling to be playing at the Nou Camp again. Lionel moved carefully at first but in the last few minutes, he came alive. He scored a simple tap-in and then dribbled fifty yards and curled a shot past the goalkeeper.

Gooooooooooooooooooooooaaaaaaaaaaaaaaaaaaalllll lllllllllllllllllll!!!!!!!!!!!!!!!

Lionel ran to the supporters with his arms outstretched. 'I'm back!' he cheered.

But Barcelona's tactics had changed since his injury. He was no longer at the centre of every attack. Martino wanted the wingers to cross the ball into the box, but what about Lionel's diagonal dribbles?

'I don't mind having less time on the ball if we're playing well, but we're not – we're losing games!' he told his dad, Jorge.

Even a Lionel hat-trick in *El Clásico* couldn't lift Barcelona. They ended the 2013/14 season without a big trophy for the first time in years. Lionel was very disappointed. Was it time for him to make a fresh start somewhere else?

But for now, his mind was on his next big challenge: the 2014 World Cup.

CHAPTER 22

ARGENTINA

'When is he going to play for his country like he plays for Barcelona?'

'Maradona won the 1986 World Cup for us – what has Messi done? Nothing!'

The people of Argentina always put a lot of pressure on their top footballers, but Lionel suffered more than most. He was the best player in the world, so why hadn't he won a World Cup or Copa América for Argentina yet? He wished that he had the answer to that question.

Since the red card on his international debut, there had been many ups and downs. He made a bright start at the 2006 World Cup in Germany but he didn't play in every game. After Olympic Gold in 2008, there were great expectations for Lionel and his teammates at the 2010 World Cup in South Africa but they almost didn't even qualify.

Diego Maradona was the new national team manager and before the 2010 tournament, he visited Lionel in Barcelona.

'You've got the Number 10 shirt now and we need you to live up to it,' Maradona told him. 'You're a very special player and you can lead this team to glory!'

Lionel tried hard but he couldn't find his best form. In the quarter-finals, Argentina were thrashed 4-0 by Germany.

'He didn't even score a single goal!' the fans complained. Some even booed him. 'At Barcelona, he scored forty-seven goals last season. Messi just doesn't care about his country!'

Spain beat the Netherlands in the final. Lionel was pleased for Xavi, Andrés, Cesc, Carles and Gerard but he couldn't help feeling jealous of his club teammates. The World Cup was the one big trophy missing from his collection. He was determined to prove his nation wrong; he *did* care.

'Brazil 2014 has to be my tournament!' Lionel told his dad.

Argentina were one of the favourites to win and Lionel was their captain. They had the advantage of playing in South America, and there were lots of superstars in the squad. Lionel felt confident as he relaxed with Sergio Agüero at the training camp.

'You, me and Ángel in attack – we can beat anyone!'

Thousands of Argentina fans had made the short journey to Brazil. They were desperate for a reason to celebrate.

When Lionel got the ball near the halfway line, Bosnia and Herzegovina thought they were safe. But in a flash, Lionel played a one-two with Gonzalo Higuaín and ran towards goal. Suddenly, Bosnia were in big trouble. A defender came out to tackle him but Lionel dribbled around him easily and aimed for the bottom corner. The ball hit the inside of the post and rolled into the net.

Goooooooooooooooooaaaaaaaaaaaaaaaaaaaalllllllllllll lllllllllllll!!!!!!!!!!!!!!!

The Argentina fans went wild. They loved Lionel when he did such amazing things.

'I've seen you score that goal a hundred times for Barca!' Javier Mascherano shouted as they hugged.

It was a great start for Lionel and he kept going. Against Iran, Argentina had lots of possession but with seconds to go, it was still 0-0. With a win, they could qualify for the second round. Ezequiel Lavezzi passed to Lionel in his favourite position on the right side of the penalty area. He was surrounded by defenders but if he couldn't dribble, he would have to shoot instead. Lionel created a bit of space and curled the ball into the top corner.

Goooooooooooooooooaaaaaaaaaaaaaaaaaaaalllllllll lllllllllllllll!!!!!!!!!!!!!!!

He ran to the fans with his arms out and a serious look on his face. He was focused on winning the World Cup for his country.

'Lionel to the rescue!' Pablo Zabaleta screamed as they celebrated.

Argentina were already through to the knockout stages but Lionel didn't want to sit on the bench for the last group match against Nigeria. 'I can rest when we've won the trophy!' he told Argentina's manager Alejandro Sabella.

Lionel scored after three minutes and just before half-time, the team won a free-kick. Everyone knew who would take it. Lionel had scored lots of free-kicks for Barcelona but it was time to do it for Argentina. There was nothing that the goalkeeper could do as the ball flew into the top corner.

Gooooooooooooooooaaaaaaaaaaaaaaaaaaaaalllllllllll llllllllllllllll!!!!!!!!!!!!!!!!!

Lionel just couldn't stop scoring. It felt so good to be playing his best football at international level at last. After sixty minutes, Sabella had to take him off.

'If you got injured today, the people of Argentina would never forgive me!' he told his superstar.

Teams defended very well against Argentina. They knew how dangerous their attackers could be and they made it very difficult for them to score. Against

Switzerland, they were minutes away from penalties.

'Come on, the goal is coming!' Lionel encouraged his teammates.

'We really need some magic,' he said to himself. He needed to play his captain's role.

Lionel dribbled forward once more, skipped past one tackle and then passed to Ángel on the right side of the penalty area. Ángel placed his shot perfectly in the bottom corner.

'Phew, I thought we'd never score!' he said as he thanked Lionel for the assist. It was a relief to make it through to the quarter-finals.

'We have to believe in ourselves,' Lionel told the other players as they prepared for the next match. 'We're a great team. If we're patient, we will always get goals!'

It only took eight minutes for Gonzalo to score for Argentina against Belgium, and so they now faced the Netherlands in the semi-finals.

'They thrashed Spain 5-1, so we have to watch out,' Sabella warned his players.

With Nigel de Jong following him all over the
pitch, Lionel struggled to create the goal that
Argentina needed. It was frustrating but he never
stopped trying. When the match went to extra-time,
Lionel gave a team-talk. He wasn't a quiet youngster
anymore. He was the team leader and everyone
listened to him.

'Lads, we've done so well to get this far. Keep
fighting – we're one step away from the World Cup
Final!'

The match went to penalties and Lionel went
first for his country. He stayed calm and sent the
goalkeeper the wrong way.

'Come on!' he shouted as he ran back to the
halfway line. He was buzzing with adrenaline.

When Maxi Rodríguez scored the winning spot-
kick, Lionel ran as fast as he could into the big team
huddle. He was so proud of their achievement.

'We're in the World Cup Final!' he cried. He
couldn't believe it. Was his dream about to come
true?

Germany had beaten Brazil 7-1 in the other semi-

final – it would be a very tough match but Lionel
stayed positive.

'It doesn't matter what happened before,' he told
his teammates. 'This is the final – anything could
happen.'

Sabella wanted revenge. 'Germany beat us 4-0 in
2010 – let's show them how much we've improved
since then!'

Lionel led his team out on to the pitch at Rio
de Janeiro's Maracanã Stadium. As they played
Argentina's national anthem, he focused on the
match ahead. The beautiful, gold trophy was only
metres away from him.

'I need to win it!' he told himself.

Again, Lionel was marked very closely. He didn't
get much of the ball but his runs created space for
his teammates. The Flea never stopped moving.
After twenty minutes, Gonzalo missed a great
chance to score. Ten minutes later, Gonzalo scored
but he was offside.

'Keep going!' Lionel urged his strike partner.

The match went to extra-time and the Argentina

players were exhausted. When Mario Götze scored to win the final for Germany, Lionel felt sick. After all their hard work, it was heartbreaking to lose in the final.

'We were so close!' Lionel thought to himself as he walked around the pitch. He had won the award for Best Player at the World Cup but that wasn't the prize that he wanted. With tears in his eyes, he watched the German celebrations.

'You'll only be thirty-one at the 2018 World Cup,' Jorge said a few days later, trying to comfort his son. 'You might even be playing in 2022!'

Lionel nodded. He had to win something with Argentina before he retired. He needed to make his country proud.

CHAPTER 23

MSN

'Why do they keep saying that I'm past my best?' Lionel complained to Gerard. He was fed up with people saying negative things about him. 'I'm only twenty-seven!'

'Don't ever listen to the media!' Gerard told him. 'We know that you're still the best player in the world. You just need to prove it on the football pitch this season.'

There were more changes back at Barcelona. Their third musketeer, Cesc, had moved to Chelsea and another new superstar had arrived at the Nou Camp: the Uruguayan striker Luis Suárez.

'You, Neymar and Suárez in the same team – do you think it can work?' Jorge asked him.

Lionel nodded eagerly. 'Of course! It's going to be great.'

Barcelona's new manager was Luis Enrique, the former club captain who played in the Porto match when young Lionel made his debut. Ten years later, they were working together again.

'Watching you that day, I knew that you'd be a superstar!' Enrique said with a smile. He had invited Lionel to his office to discuss his role for the new season.

'Here's my challenge: I have three of the best attackers in the world and I need to get them playing well together in the same team. I know – it's a very nice challenge to have! My plan is to play you in a free role just behind Neymar and Luis. Are you happy with that?'

Lionel nodded.

'Good but I want you to keep scoring lots of goals, okay?'

Lionel smiled. 'Don't worry about that!'

Soon, the whole football world was talking about 'MSN' – Messi, Suárez, Neymar.

Neymar dribbled in from the left and passed to Luis. Luis flicked the ball through for the one-two and Lionel was already making his run to the back-post to tap in Neymar's cross.

Gooooooooooooooooaaaaaaaaaaaaaaaaaaaaallllllllllllll llllllllllllllllll!!!!!!!!!!!!!!!!!

'It's like we've been playing together for years!' Lionel joked as the three superstars hugged.

'Don't forget about me!' Andrés shouted as he joined them.

Against the La Liga champions Atlético Madrid, Neymar scored the first and Luis got the second.

'I set you both up – now I need to get a goal of my own!' Lionel laughed. He was really enjoying his football again. With a few minutes to go, he finally got his goal. 'MSN' were simply unstoppable.

'We're going to win the Treble again this year!' Gerard predicted.

In the Champions League semi-final in May 2015, Barcelona faced Bayern Munich. Their manager was

Pep Guardiola, the man who had helped to turn
Lionel into a superstar.

'He knows everything about me so their defenders
will be prepared,' Lionel said to his strike partners.

'Well he's never coached me!' Neymar replied.

'Or me!' Luis added.

In the second half, Lionel found a bit of space in
his favourite zone – on the right, just outside the
penalty area. Before the defenders could react, the
ball was in the back of the net.

*Gooooooooooooooooaaaaaaaaaaaaaaallllllllllllllllllll
lllllllll!!!!!!!!!!!!!!!!!*

Lionel was delighted with his crucial strike. He ran
to the fans with his fists pumping like a boxer.

'They know how to stop you but they can't,' Luis
cheered. 'You're just too good!'

Just a few minutes later, Lionel dribbled at Bayern
defender Jérôme Boateng. He cut inside on his left
foot as usual but in a flash, he nutmegged Boateng
and lifted the ball over the keeper with his right foot.

*Gooooooooooooooooaaaaaaaaaaaaaaallllllllllllllllllll
lllllllllllll!!!!!!!!!!!!!!!!!*

'That's the best goal I've ever seen!' Neymar screamed as he jumped on top of the pile of Barcelona players.

There was still time for Lionel to set up Neymar to make it 3-0. It was a night that he would never, ever forget. Lionel was on fire.

'I think you might be better than ever right now!' Enrique told him happily.

That same month, May 2015, Lionel scored the winner as Barcelona beat Atlético Madrid 1-0 to secure the La Liga title. Two weeks later, he scored twice as they beat Athletic Bilbao 3-1 to win the Copa del Rey. Gerard was right; if they could beat Juventus in the Champions League final, they would win the treble.

With one game left in the season, MSN had already scored 120 goals between them.

'We're officially the best front three ever!' Luis reported.

Lionel couldn't wait to play in yet another big European final. He was determined to get a proper hat-trick of winner's medals. But after sixty-five minutes, the score was still 1-1. He had some work to do.

Lionel ran through the middle, dribbled past one defender and then hit a powerful shot. The ball swerved through the air and the keeper could only push it away. Luis was ready for the rebound. 2-1!

Lionel and Neymar chased after their strike partner as he ran around the pitch in Berlin. Eventually, they caught up with Luis and they celebrated in style.

With seconds to go, Lionel played a brilliant through-ball to Neymar. The Brazilian passed to Luis, who passed back to him. The tired Juventus defenders couldn't cope with their brilliant teamwork. Neymar fired the ball into the net. 3-1!

'MSN' to the rescue again! Lionel hadn't scored but he had been involved in everything. He finished an incredible year by winning his fifth Ballon d'Or trophy.

What next for the best player in the world? In the 2015/16 season, 'MSN' did it all over again. They scored 131 goals together and Barcelona won the La Liga and Copa del Rey double.

But then came Copa América, and for a brief period, the three players would be playing against each other, in their respective international teams.

'For the next few weeks, we're enemies, not friends!' Lionel told Neymar and Luis excitedly; Brazil and Uruguay would be two of Argentina's biggest rivals.

Argentina made it to the final in 2016, facing Chile for the second year running. Chile had been victorious the previous year, so Lionel was desperate for revenge and a first Copa América title.

When the match went to penalties, Lionel volunteered to go first for his country. He looked calm and confident as he stepped up but his shot went flying over the crossbar. He put his hands to his face.

'I can't believe I did that!' he said to Javier Mascherano. 'I'm normally good at taking penalties.'

Argentina lost and Lionel was so disappointed that he retired from international football. The nation was shocked. They couldn't lose their captain and biggest superstar. A big 'Don't go, Leo' campaign began.

'Are you sure about this?' his dad asked him. 'Don't you want to win the World Cup?'

Jorge knew how much Lionel wanted to win *everything*. It was that competitive spirit, combined with hard work and incredible skills, which had taken him all the way from street football in Rosario to Barcelona and eight La Liga titles, four Champions League trophies, five Ballon d'Ors and an Olympic gold medal.

With the help of his family, teammates and coaches, Lionel had overcome his growth problems to become the best footballer in the world by the age of twenty-two. He was now twenty-eight but there were still goals that he wanted to achieve.

Just two months later, Lionel was back in the Argentina squad.

'We've got the 2018 World Cup to win!' he told his teammates. The Flea had more defences to terrorise and he couldn't wait.

Turn the page for a sneak preview of
another brilliant football story by
Matt and Tom Oldfield. . .

ANDRÉS INIESTA

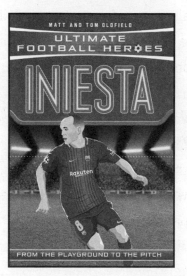

Available now!

CHAPTER 1

EL CAPITAN

In many ways, it was just like any other game day. Andrés arrived at the Nou Camp three hours before kick-off and, still in his tracksuit, went to look at the pitch. It looked glorious – like an inviting green carpet. The sun was shining and the stands would soon be full of cheering Barcelona fans.

Andrés darted back inside, waving to some of the Nou Camp staff and then stopping to sign autographs for two young boys, one wearing a Lionel Messi shirt, the other with Andrés' own 'INIESTA 8' on the back. He paused outside the Barcelona dressing room, taking in the moment. It was the start of a new season and a new era. 'Here we go,' he said to himself.

He saw that all of his kit was already laid out

neatly. No matter how many games he played, he never got tired of seeing his name on that famous Barcelona shirt.

Then he spotted the new item, tucked away on a little shelf above his head. The red and yellow captain's armband. It was now his. So many of the leaders who had guided Andrés during his early days in the first team had since moved on. Now *he* was leading the charge.

'El capitán!' a familiar voice called out.

Andrés turned to see Leo Messi grinning at him from across the room.

'No pressure,' Leo said. 'You just have to lead us to a repeat of last year's Treble-winning season!'

'Thanks, Leo!' Andrés replied, laughing. He was happy to joke about it, but deep down he knew he had big shoes to fill. His teammates would be looking to him more than ever for inspiration. And the expectations were always so high at Barcelona.

Andrés took out his phone and checked his messages. He saw a text message from his good friend Victor Valdés, who he had known since his earliest days at La Masia, the Barcelona academy.

The message read: 'Andrés, today's the day! Your first game as captain of Barcelona. You're going to be great. I still remember the day you arrived at La Masia – what a journey!'

Andrés got kind words everywhere he turned that afternoon as he prepared for the game – a home friendly against Roma. Everyone wanted to talk about the new season and, most of all, his new role.

'Andrés, I remember watching you play when you were this tall,' a Nou Camp worker told him, indicating his own waist. 'And now here you are, leading out the team. I always said you would be captain one day. I just knew it.'

'Don't listen to him,' another worker interrupted, laughing and wagging his finger. 'He says that about every young player who arrives at La Masia.'

'No I don't!'

Andrés smiled. He was beginning to realise that this was an even bigger day than he had thought. He had expected the pre-game warm-up to feel the same as it always did. After all, he had been the stand-in captain plenty of times last season. But he quickly saw that this was different. He wasn't just one of the senior players anymore; he had to be the leader and he had to make sure that everyone was focused on doing their jobs.

Even though Andrés had never been a big talker on the pitch, he went to each of his teammates to pump them up and encourage them. He finished by joining Luis Suárez and Javier Mascherano to pass the ball around.

'Don't worry, Andrés,' Luis said, putting an arm on his teammate's shoulder. 'I've got my scoring boots on. We'll make sure you get off to a winning start as captain.'

Andrés smiled. 'That's good because Leo and Neymar were both just telling me that they were going to score more goals than you this season,' he said, with a wink. He was making it up, but he knew it would make Luis play even better.

'Keep it tight at the back,' he said, turning to Javier and sounding serious again. 'Look for me. I'll always be available for a pass.'

Andrés had time for two more stretches and then he jogged back up the tunnel to the dressing room, with his heart thumping faster than usual.

Barcelona manager Luis Enrique gave the team his last instructions, keeping it relaxed for the pre-season game. He finished by looking over at Andrés and invited his new captain to add his message for the team.

Andrés smiled shyly. 'Well, you all know how much I love making big speeches,' he joked. His teammates cheered. They were well aware that Andrés preferred to let his feet do the talking. 'Let's carry on where we left off last season,' he said. 'Play like champions. This is the first step towards defending our trophies.'

As he stood in the tunnel with his teammates behind him, the pitch ahead of him and the Barcelona fans singing loudly, Andrés smiled to himself. Even after all the trophies and awards, he sometimes had to pinch himself to believe that he was really living his dream of playing for Barcelona.

He re-positioned the armband one last time and closed his eyes. He took a deep breath and thought about everything it had taken to reach this special moment.

LIONEL MESSI HONOURS

Barcelona

🏆 La Liga: 2004–05, 2005–06, 2008–09, 2009–10, 2010–11, 2012–13, 2014–15, 2015–16

🏆 Copa del Rey: 2008–09, 2011–12, 2014–15, 2015–16

🏆 Champions League: 2005–06, 2008–09, 2010–11, 2014–15

🏆 FIFA Club World Cup: 2009, 2011, 2015

Argentina

🏆 FIFA U-20 World Cup: 2005

🏆 Olympic Gold Medal: 2008

Individual

🏆 FIFA Under-20 World Cup Golden Ball: 2005

- 🏆 FIFA Under-20 World Cup Golden Shoe: 2005
- 🏆 Golden Boy: 2005
- 🏆 FIFPro Young World Player of the Year: 2006, 2007, 2008
- 🏆 UEFA Goal of the Season: 2006–07, 2014–15, 2015–16
- 🏆 Copa América Best Young Player: 2007
- 🏆 FIFA FIFPro World XI: 2007, 2008, 2009, 2010, 2011, 2012, 2013, 2014, 2015, 2016
- 🏆 UEFA Team of the Year: 2008, 2009, 2010, 2011, 2012, 2014, 2015, 2016
- 🏆 UEFA Champions League Top Goalscorer: 2008–09, 2009–10, 2010–11, 2011–12, 2014–15
- 🏆 FIFA Ballon d'Or: 2009, 2010, 2011, 2012, 2015
- 🏆 Best Player in La Liga: 2009, 2010, 2011, 2012, 2013, 2015
- 🏆 La Liga Top Goalscorer: 2009–10, 2011–12, 2012–13
- 🏆 European Golden Shoe: 2010, 2012, 2013
- 🏆 UEFA Best Player in Europe: 2011, 2015
- 🏆 FIFA World Cup Golden Ball: 2014

MESSI

10 THE FACTS

NAME:
Lionel Andrés Messi

DATE OF BIRTH:
24 June 1987

AGE: 29

PLACE OF BIRTH:
Rosario

NATIONALITY: Argentina

BEST FRIEND: Sergio Agüero

CURRENT CLUB: Barcelona

POSITION: RW

THE STATS

Height (cm):	170
Club appearances:	614
Club goals:	517
Club trophies:	29
International appearances:	117
International goals:	58
International trophies:	1
Ballon d'Ors:	5

★ ★ ★ **HERO RATING: 95** ★ ★ ★

GREATEST MOMENTS

1 MAY 2005,
BARCELONA 2-0 ALBACETE

Lionel made his Barcelona debut back in 2004 but by May 2005, he was still looking for his first goal. With five minutes to go, Ronaldinho chipped the ball over the defence and Lionel lobbed the goalkeeper with an amazing side-foot finish. That goal made him Barcelona's youngest ever scorer. A superstar was born!

2 — 10 MARCH 2007, BARCELONA 3-3 REAL MADRID

When Ronaldinho and Deco started to lose their magic, Barcelona needed a new hero to lead the team to glory. In the 2007 *Clásico* against Real Madrid, Lionel became that hero. He scored his first ever professional hat-trick to keep Barça in the game and in the Spanish title race.

3 — 18 APRIL 2007, BARCELONA 5-2 GETAFE

This was the match when Lionel really became 'The New Maradona'. He started an incredible run from inside his own half. After dribbling past four defenders at full speed, Lionel coolly took the ball round the goalkeeper and scored. It looked like Diego Maradona's wonder-goal for Argentina against England, only maybe even better!

4 28 MAY 2011, BARCELONA 3-1 MANCHESTER UNITED

Lionel was brilliant in both of Barcelona's Champions League Final wins over Manchester United but in 2011, he was the best player on the planet. First, he scored the goals to beat Cristiano Ronaldo's Real Madrid in the semi-final, and then he was the star of the show in the final.

5 6 JUNE 2015, BARCELONA 3-1 JUVENTUS

Lionel didn't score in this Champions League Final but he played a crucial role yet again. His powerful shot led to Luis Suarez's goal and then he started the amazing counter-attack for Neymar's goal. That night was 'MSN', Barcelona's superstar strikeforce, at their very best.

PLAY LIKE YOUR HEROES

THE LIONEL MESSI
DRIBBLE

STEP 1: Dribble down the right wing with your left foot in a tricky one-on-one situation.

STEP 2: Move your body to the left, as if you're going to cut inside.

STEP 3: Bring your left foot down a little to the left of the ball (don't touch it yet!).

STEP 4: As the defenders moves to that side, quickly shift your body back to the right.

STEP 5: As you do that, shift the ball from your left foot to your right foot.

STEP 6: Kick the ball forward with your right foot and speed away as fast as you can.

STEP 7: Dribble past three more defenders and score a wonder-goal!

TEST YOUR KNOWLEDGE

QUESTIONS

1. What was the name of Lionel's first football club?

2. Who does Lionel dedicate his goals to when he points up at the sky?

3. Who was Lionel's strike partner in Newell Old Boys' Team of '87?

4. Who introduced Lionel to Antonella?

5. How old was Lionel when he left Argentina and moved to Barcelona?

6. When and where did Lionel first meet Sergio Agüero?

7. How old was Lionel when he made his Barcelona

debut and who were the opponents?

8. Which Brazilian superstar took Lionel under his wing in his early years at Barcelona?

9. Which two friends from *La Masia* left Barcelona but then came back to play with Lionel again?

10. How many different shirt numbers has Lionel worn at Barcelona?

11. How many Champions League winner's medals does Lionel have?

Answers below. . . No cheating!

1. *Grandoli.* 2. *Celia, his grandmother* 3. *Diego Rovira.* 4. *His friend, Lucas Scaglia, who is Antonella's cousin.* 5. *13* 6. *In June 2005 at the Under-20 World Cup in Holland. Together, they won the tournament.* 7. *Lionel was 16 and the match was a friendly against Porto.* 8. *Ronaldinho* 9. *Cesc Fàbregas and Gerard Piqué* 10. *Four (14, 30, 19, 10)* 11. *Four (2006, 2009, 2011 and 2015)*

HAVE YOU GOT THEM ALL?

ULTIMATE FOOTBALL HEROES

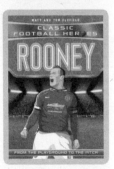